JAVA™ LOOK AND FEEL
DESIGN GUIDELINES

Please send your email feedback to us at jlfguide@sun.com

JAVA™ LOOK AND FEEL DESIGN GUIDELINES

Sun Microsystems, Inc.

Addison-Wesley

An imprint of Addison Wesley Longman, Inc.

Reading, Massachusetts • Harlow, England • Menlo Park, California
Berkeley, California • Don Mills, Ontario • Sydney • Bonn
Amsterdam • Tokyo • Mexico City

The publisher offers discounts on this book when ordered in quantity for special sales. For more information, please contact:

Corporate & Professional Publishing Group
Addison-Wesley Publishing Company
One Jacob Way
Reading, Massachusetts 01867

Text printed on recycled and acid-free paper

ISBN 0-201-61585-1
1 2 3 4 5 6 7 8 9-MA-99989796
First Printing, June 1999

Please Recycle

Adobe PostScript™

CONTENTS

Preface   xix

Part I: Overview   1

Chapter 1: The Java Look and Feel   3
Fundamentals of the Java Look and Feel   3
Visual Tour of the Java Look and Feel   4
    MetalEdit Application   5
    Retirement Savings Calculator Applet   10

Chapter 2: The Java Foundation Classes   15
Java Development Kit   15
    Java Foundation Classes   15
    JDK 1.1 and the Java 2 SDK   16
    Support for Accessibility   16
    Support for Internationalization   17
User Interface Components of the Java Foundation Classes   17
    Pluggable Look and Feel Architecture   17
    Example Model and Interface   18
    Client Properties   18
    Major JFC User Interface Components   19
Look and Feel Options   23
    Java Look and Feel—the Recommended Design   23
    Alternative Approaches   23
    Supplied Designs   24

Part II: Fundamental Java Application Design   25

Chapter 3: Design Considerations   27
Choosing an Application or an Applet   27
    Distribution   28
    Security Issues   28
    Placement of Applets   29
Designing for Accessibility   30
    Benefits of Accessibility   30
    Accessible Design   30

Planning for Internationalization and Localization   33
   Benefits of Global Planning   34
   Global Design   34

Chapter 4: Visual Design   39
Themes   39
   Colors   40
   Fonts   45
Capitalization of Text in the Interface   46
   Headline Capitalization in English   46
   Sentence Capitalization in English   47
Layout and Visual Alignment   47
   Between-Component Padding and Spacing Guidelines   48
   Design Grids   49
   Titled Borders for Panels   51
   Text Layout   52
Animation   54
   Progress and Delay Indication   54
   System Status Animation   55

Chapter 5: Application Graphics   57
Working With Cross-Platform Color   57
   Working With Available Colors   58
   Choosing Graphic File Formats   58
   Choosing Colors   59
   Maximizing Color Quality   60
Designing Graphics in the Java Look and Feel Style   62
Designing Icons   63
   Working With Icon Styles   63
   Drawing Icons   64
Designing Button Graphics   66
   Using Button Graphic Styles   67
   Producing the Flush 3D Effect   67
   Working With Button Borders   68
   Determining the Primary Drawing Area   68
   Drawing the Button Graphic   69
Designing Symbols   72
Designing Graphics for Corporate and Product Identity   73
   Designing Installation Screens   73
   Designing Splash Screens   73

Designing Login Splash Screens 75
Designing About Boxes 76

Chapter 6: Behavior 77
Mouse Operations 77
    Pointer Feedback 78
    Mouse-over Feedback 79
    Clicking and Selecting Objects 80
    Displaying Contextual Menus 80
Drag-and-Drop Operations 81
    Typical Drag and Drop 81
    Pointer and Destination Feedback 82
Keyboard Operations 82
    Keyboard Focus 83
    Keyboard Navigation and Activation 85
    Keyboard Shortcuts 87
    Mnemonics 88

Part III: The Components of the Java Foundation Classes 91

Chapter 7: Windows, Panes, and Frames 93
Anatomy of a Primary Window 95
Constructing Windows 97
    Primary Windows 97
    Secondary Windows 98
    Plain Windows 99
    Utility Windows 100
Organizing Windows 101
    Panels 101
    Scroll Panes 102
    Tabbed Panes 104
    Split Panes 106
Working With Multiple Document Interfaces 108
    Internal Frames 108
    Palettes 110

Chapter 8: Dialog Boxes 111
Modal and Modeless Dialog Boxes 112
Dialog Box Design 112
    Tab Traversal Order 114
    Spacing in Dialog Boxes 115

Command Buttons in Dialog Boxes   115
Default Command Buttons   118
Common Dialog Boxes   120
Find Dialog Boxes   120
Login Dialog Boxes   120
Preferences Dialog Boxes   120
Print Dialog Boxes   121
Progress Dialog Boxes   121
Alert Boxes   122
Info Alert Boxes   123
Warning Alert Boxes   124
Error Alert Boxes   124
Question Alert Boxes   125
Color Choosers   126

Chapter 9: Menus and Toolbars   129
Menu Elements   130
Menu Bars   130
Drop-down Menus   131
Submenus   132
Menu Items   132
Checkbox Menu Items   135
Radio Button Menu Items   135
Separators   136
Common Menus   136
Typical File Menu   137
Object Menu   137
Typical Edit Menu   138
Typical Format Menu   138
View Menu   139
Typical Help Menu   139
Contextual Menus   139
Toolbars   140
Toolbar Placement   141
Draggable Toolbars   141
Toolbar Buttons   142
Tool Tips   145

Chapter 10: Basic Controls   147
Command Buttons   148
   Default Command Buttons   149
   Combining Graphics With Text in Command Buttons   150
   Using Ellipses in Command Buttons   150
   Command Button Spacing   151
   Command Button Padding   151
Toggle Buttons   152
   Independent Choice   152
   Exclusive Choice   153
Checkboxes   154
   Checkbox Spacing   154
Radio Buttons   155
   Radio Button Spacing   156
Combo Boxes   156
   Noneditable Combo Boxes   157
   Editable Combo Boxes   158
Sliders   159
Progress Bars   160

Chapter 11: Text Components   163
Labels   164
   Labels That Identify Controls   164
   Labels That Communicate Status and Other Information   166
Text Fields   167
   Noneditable Text Fields   167
   Editable Text Fields   167
Password Fields   168
Text Areas   169
Editor Panes   170
   Default Editor Kit   170
   Styled Text Editor Kit   170
   RTF Editor Kit   171
   HTML Editor Kit   172

Chapter 12: Lists, Tables, and Trees   173
Lists   173
   Scrolling   174
   Selection Models for Lists   174

Tables   176
    Table Appearance   177
    Table Scrolling   177
    Column Reordering   177
    Column Resizing   178
    Row Sorting   179
    Selection Models for Tables   180
Tree Views   187
    Lines in Tree Views   188
    Graphics in Tree Views   189
    Editing in Tree Views   189

Appendix A: Keyboard Navigation, Activation, and Selection   191
Checkboxes   192
Combo Boxes   192
Command Buttons   193
Desktop Panes and Internal Frames   193
Dialog Boxes   194
HTML Editor Kits   194
Lists   195
Menus   196
Radio Buttons   196
Scrollbars   197
Sliders   197
Split Panes   198
Tabbed Panes   198
Tables   199
Text Areas and Default and Styled Text Editor Kits   200
Text Fields   202
Toggle Buttons   202
Tool Tips   203
Toolbars   203
Tree Views   203

Glossary   205

Index   219

FIGURES

FIGURE 1   Consistent Use of the Flush 3D Style   3

FIGURE 2   Consistent Use of the Drag Texture   4

FIGURE 3   Role of the Color Model in Compatibility   4

FIGURE 4   Typical Desktop With Applications on the Microsoft Windows Platform   5

FIGURE 5   Document Window on Three Platforms   6

FIGURE 6   Example Menu Bar   6

FIGURE 7   Example Drop-down Menus   7

FIGURE 8   Example Toolbar   8

FIGURE 9   Example Editor Pane   8

FIGURE 10   Example Dialog Boxes on Microsoft Windows, Macintosh, and CDE Platforms   9

FIGURE 11   Example Alert Boxes on CDE, Microsoft Windows, and Macintosh Platforms   10

FIGURE 12   Applet on an HTML Page in a Browser (Exploded View)   11

FIGURE 13   Retirement Savings Calculator Applet   12

FIGURE 14   Java Foundation Classes for JDK 1.1 and the Java 2 SDK   16

FIGURE 15   Structure of the JFC Components   17

FIGURE 16   Pluggable Look and Feel Architecture of a Slider   18

FIGURE 17   Environments for Applications and Applets   27

FIGURE 18   Mnemonics in a Dialog Box   32

FIGURE 19   English and Japanese Notification Dialog Boxes   34

FIGURE 20   Cancel Buttons in English, German, and Japanese   35

FIGURE 21   Correct Word Order in English But Not in French   36

FIGURE 22   Correct Word Order in Both English and French   36

FIGURE 23   Primary Colors in Default Color Theme   41

FIGURE 24   Secondary Colors in Default Color Theme   42

FIGURE 25   Green Color Theme   44

FIGURE 26   High-Contrast Color Theme   44

FIGURE 27   Perceived and Actual Spacing of Active and Inactive Components   48

FIGURE 28   Grid With Horizontal Divisions   49

FIGURE 29   Vertical Separation of Command Buttons   50

FIGURE 30   Vertical Separation of Component Groups   51

FIGURE 31   Spacing for a Panel With Titled Border   51

FIGURE 32   Label Orientation   53

FIGURE 33   Animation in a Progress Dialog Box   55

FIGURE 34   Adding a Pattern to Avoid Coarse Dithering Patterns   61

FIGURE 35   Two Families of Icons   63

FIGURE 36   Button Graphics for a Toolbar and a Tool Palette   67

FIGURE 37   Flush 3D Effect in a Button Graphic   67

FIGURE 38   Button Graphics With Borders   68

FIGURE 39   Primary Drawing Area in Buttons   68

FIGURE 40   Maximum-Size Button Graphics   69

FIGURE 41   Symbols   72

FIGURE 42   Splash Screen for MetalEdit   74

FIGURE 43   Login Splash Screen for MetalMail   75

FIGURE 44   About Box for MetalEdit   76

FIGURE 45   Cross-Platform Mouse Buttons and Their Default Assignments   78

FIGURE 46   Contextual Menu for a Text Selection   81

FIGURE 47   Keyboard Focus Indicated by Rectangular Border   84

FIGURE 48   Keyboard Focus Indicated by Blinking Bar at Insertion Point   84

FIGURE 49   Keyboard Focus Indicated by Colored Background   85

FIGURE 50   Keyboard Focus Indicated by Drag Texture   85

FIGURE 51   Edit Menu With Keyboard Shortcuts and Mnemonics   87

FIGURE 52   File Menu With Mnemonics and Keyboard Shortcuts   89

FIGURE 53   Primary, Utility, Plain, and Secondary Windows   93

FIGURE 54   Scroll Pane, Tabbed Pane, Split Pane, and Internal Frame   94

FIGURE 55   Components Contained in a Primary Window   95

FIGURE 56   Anatomy of a Primary Window   96

FIGURE 57   Top-Level Containers   97

FIGURE 58   Primary Window on the Microsoft Windows Platform   98

FIGURE 59   Alert Box on the Macintosh Platform   99

FIGURE 60   Plain Window Used as the Basis for a Splash Screen   99

FIGURE 61   Utility Window   100

FIGURE 62   Lower-Level Containers   101

FIGURE 63   Scroll Pane in a Document Window   102

FIGURE 64   Vertical and Horizontal Scrollbars   103

FIGURE 65   Swatches Content Pane in the JFC Color Chooser   105

FIGURE 66   RGB Content Pane in the JFC Color Chooser   105

FIGURE 67   Split Pane (Horizontal Orientation)   106

FIGURE 68   Zoom Buttons in a Split Pane (Vertical Orientation)   107

FIGURE 69   Nested Split Panes   108

FIGURE 70   Internal Frames in an MDI Application   109

FIGURE 71   Minimized Internal Frame   109

FIGURE 72   Palette Window   110

FIGURE 73   Dialog Box and Alert Box   111

FIGURE 74   Sample Dialog Box   113

FIGURE 75   Tab Traversal Order in the Sample Dialog Box   114

FIGURE 76   Spacing Between the Border and Components of a Dialog Box   115

FIGURE 77   Dialog Box With a Close Button   116

FIGURE 78   Dialog Box With OK, Cancel, and Help Buttons   117

FIGURE 79   Dialog Box With Apply, Reset, and Close Buttons   118

FIGURE 80   Dialog Box With a Default Command Button   119

FIGURE 81   Alert Box Without a Default Button   119

FIGURE 82   Sample Find Dialog Box   120

FIGURE 83   Sample Login Dialog Box   120

FIGURE 84   Sample Preferences Dialog Box   121

FIGURE 85   Sample Progress Dialog Box   122

FIGURE 86   Standard Components in an Alert Box   123

FIGURE 87   Info Alert Box   123

FIGURE 88   Warning Alert Box   124

FIGURE 89   Error Alert Box   125

FIGURE 90   Question Alert Box   126

FIGURE 91   Standard Color Chooser   126

FIGURE 92   Drop-down Menu, Submenu, Contextual Menu, and Toolbar   129

FIGURE 93   Menu Elements   130

FIGURE 94   Menu Item With Its Submenu   132

FIGURE 95   Typical Menu Items   133

FIGURE 96   Checkbox Menu Items   135

FIGURE 97   Radio Button Menu Items   135

FIGURE 98   Separators in a Menu   136

FIGURE 99   Typical File Menu   137

FIGURE 100   Typical Edit Menu   138

FIGURE 101   Typical Format Menu   138

FIGURE 102   Typical Help Menu   139

FIGURE 103   Contextual Menu   140

FIGURE 104   Horizontal Toolbar   140

FIGURE 105   Outline of a Toolbar Being Dragged   142

FIGURE 106   Toolbar in a Separate Window   142

FIGURE 107   Toolbar Button Spacing   143

FIGURE 108   Mouse-over Border on a Toolbar Button   144

FIGURE 109   Toolbar Button With a Drop-down Menu   144

FIGURE 110   Tool Tip for a Toolbar Button   145

FIGURE 111   Tool Tip for a Slider   145

FIGURE 112   Tool Tip on an Area Within a Graphic   146

FIGURE 113   Buttons, Combo Box, Slider, and Progress Bar   147

FIGURE 114   Command Buttons   148

FIGURE 115   Toolbar Buttons   148

FIGURE 116   Available, Pressed, and Unavailable Command Buttons   149

FIGURE 117   Default and Nondefault Command Buttons   149

FIGURE 118   Command Buttons Containing Both Text and Graphics   150

FIGURE 119   Command Button Text With Centered Text   151

FIGURE 120   Spacing in Command Button Groups   151

FIGURE 121   Independent Toggle Buttons in a Toolbar   152

FIGURE 122   Standard Separation of Exclusive Toggle Buttons   153

FIGURE 123   Grouped Toggle Buttons With a Label   153

FIGURE 124   Checkboxes   154

FIGURE 125   Checkbox Spacing   155

FIGURE 126   Radio Buttons   155

FIGURE 127   Radio Button Spacing   156

FIGURE 128   Combo Box Display   157

FIGURE 129   Noneditable Combo Box   158

FIGURE 130   Editable Combo Box   158

FIGURE 131   Nonfilling Slider   159

FIGURE 132   Filling Slider   160

FIGURE 133   Progress Bar   160

FIGURE 134   Text Inside a Progress Bar   161

FIGURE 135   Text Components   163

FIGURE 136   Label That Describes the Use of a Slider   164

FIGURE 137   Label That Describes a Radio Button Group   164

FIGURE 138   Active and Inactive Labels   165

FIGURE 139   Spacing Between a Label and a Component   165

FIGURE 140   Label With a Mnemonic   166

FIGURE 141   Labels That Clarify the Meaning of a Progress Bar   166

FIGURE 142   Noneditable Text Field   167

FIGURE 143   Editable Text Field With Blinking Bar   167

FIGURE 144   Editable Text Field With Selected Text   168

FIGURE 145   Password Field   169

FIGURE 146   Text Area   169

FIGURE 147   Text Area in a Scroll Pane   170

FIGURE 148   Styled Text Editor Kit   171

FIGURE 149   RTF Editor Kit   171

FIGURE 150   HTML Editor Kit   172

FIGURE 151   List, Table, and Tree View   173

FIGURE 152   Nonexclusive List   173

FIGURE 153   Single-Item Selection in a List   174

FIGURE 154   Range of Selected Items in a List   175

FIGURE 155   Multiple Ranges of Selected Items in a List   175

FIGURE 156   Table in a Scroll Pane   176

FIGURE 157   Reordering Columns by Dragging a Column Header   178

FIGURE 158   Row Sorting in an Email Application   179

FIGURE 159   Single-Cell Selection   181

FIGURE 160   Range of Selected Cells   181

FIGURE 161   Single-Row Selection   182

FIGURE 162   Range of Selected Rows   183

FIGURE 163   Multiple Ranges of Selected Rows   184

FIGURE 164   Single-Column Selection   185

FIGURE 165   Range of Selected Columns   185

FIGURE 166   Multiple Ranges of Selected Columns   186

FIGURE 167   Tree View With Top-Level Lines   187

FIGURE 168   Tree View With Hierarchy Lines   188

TABLES

TABLE 1   Names and Appearance of the JFC User Interface Components   19

TABLE 2   Colors of the Default Java Look and Feel Theme   43

TABLE 3   Type Styles Defined by the Java Look and Feel   45

TABLE 4   Remappings of a Blurred Graphic   60

TABLE 5   Variations in Reproduction of 8-Bit Color   61

TABLE 6   Examples of Application Graphics   62

TABLE 7   Pointer Types Available in JDK 1.1 and the Java 2 SDK   79

TABLE 8   Common Navigation and Activation Keys   86

TABLE 9   Common Keyboard Shortcuts   88

TABLE 10   Common Mnemonics   90

TABLE 11   Background Color of Table Cells   177

TABLE 12   Table Resize Options   178

TABLE 13   Keyboard Operation for Checkboxes   192

TABLE 14   Keyboard Operations for Combo Boxes   192

TABLE 15   Keyboard Operations for Command Buttons   193

TABLE 16   Keyboard Operations for Desktop Panes and Internal Frames   193

TABLE 17   Keyboard Operations for Dialog Boxes   194

TABLE 18   Keyboard Operations for HTML Panes   194

TABLE 19   Keyboard Operations for Lists   195

TABLE 20   Keyboard Operations for Menus   196

TABLE 21   Keyboard Operation for Radio Buttons   196

TABLE 22   Keyboard Operations for Scrollbars   197

TABLE 23   Keyboard Operations for Sliders   197

TABLE 24   Keyboard Operations for Split Panes   198

TABLE 25   Keyboard Operations for Tabbed Panes   198

TABLE 26   Keyboard Operations for Tables   199

TABLE 27   Keyboard Operations for Text Areas and Default and Styled Text Editor Kits   200

TABLE 28   Keyboard Operations for Text Fields   202

TABLE 29   Keyboard Operation for Toggle Buttons   202

TABLE 30   Keyboard Operations for Tool Tips   203

TABLE 31   Keyboard Operations for Toolbars   203

TABLE 32   Keyboard Operations for Tree Views   203

PREFACE

Java Look and Feel Design Guidelines provides essential information for anyone involved in creating cross-platform applications and applets in the Java™ programming language. In particular, this book offers design guidelines for software that uses the Java™ Foundation Classes (JFC) together with the Java look and feel.

Who Should Use This Book

Although the human interface designer and the software developer might well be the same person, the two jobs require different tasks, skills, and tools. Primarily, this book addresses the **designer** who chooses the interface components, lays them out in a set of views, and designs the user interaction model for an application. (Unless specified otherwise, this book uses "application" to refer to both applets and applications.) This book should also prove useful for developers, technical writers, graphic artists, production and marketing specialists, and testers who participate in the creation of Java applications and applets.

Java Look and Feel Design Guidelines focuses on design issues and human-computer interaction in the context of the Java look and feel. It also attempts to provide a common vocabulary for designers, developers, and other professionals. If you require more information about technical aspects of the Java Foundation Classes, visit the Java Technology and Swing Connection web sites at `http://java.sun.com` and `http://java.sun.com/products/jfc`.

The guidelines provided in this book are appropriate for applications and applets that run on personal computers and network computers. They do not address the needs of software that runs on consumer electronic devices.

What Is in This Book

Java Look and Feel Design Guidelines includes the following chapters:

Chapter 1, "The Java Look and Feel," introduces key design concepts and visual elements underlying the Java look and feel and offers a quick visual tour of an application and an applet designed with the JFC components and the Java look and feel.

Chapter 2, "The Java Foundation Classes," provides an overview of the Java™ Development Kit and the Java Foundation Classes, introduces the JFC components, discusses the concept of pluggable look and feel designs, and describes the currently available look and feel options.

Chapter 3, "Design Considerations," discusses some of the fundamental challenges of designing Java look and feel applications and applets and of providing for accessibility, internationalization, and localization.

Chapter 4, "Visual Design," suggests ways to use the Java look and feel theme mechanism to change colors and fonts, provides guidelines for the capitalization of text in the interface, and gives recommendations for layout and visual alignment.

Chapter 5, "Application Graphics," discusses the use of cross-platform color, the creation of graphics that suit the Java look and feel, and the use of graphics to enhance corporate and product identity.

Chapter 6, "Behavior," tells how users of Java look and feel applications utilize the mouse, keyboard, and screen and provides guidelines regarding user input and human-computer interaction, including drag-and-drop operations.

Chapter 7, "Windows, Panes, and Frames," discusses and makes recommendations for the use of primary, secondary, plain, and utility windows as well as panels, scroll panes, tabbed panes, split panes, and internal frames.

Chapter 8, "Dialog Boxes," describes dialog boxes and alert boxes, sets standards for dialog box design, and provides examples of typical dialog boxes in Java look and feel applications.

Chapter 9, "Menus and Toolbars," defines and gives guidelines for the use of drop-down menus, contextual menus, toolbars, and tool tips and provides examples of typical menus in Java look and feel applications.

Chapter 10, "Basic Controls," covers the use of controls such as command buttons, toggle buttons, checkboxes, radio buttons, sliders, and combo boxes; it also describes progress bars and provides suggestions for their use.

Chapter 11, "Text Components," explains and makes recommendations for the use of the JFC components that control the display and editing of text: labels, text fields, text areas, and editor panes.

Chapter 12, "Lists, Tables, and Trees," discusses and makes recommendations for the use of lists, tables, and tree views.

Appendix A, **"Keyboard Navigation, Activation, and Selection,"** contains tables that specify keyboard operations for the components of the Java Foundation Classes.

Glossary defines important words and phrases found in this book. Glossary terms appear in boldface throughout the book.

What Is Not in This Book

This book does not provide detailed discussions of human interface design principles or the design process, nor does it present much general information about usability testing.

For authoritative explications of human interface design principles and the design process, see *Macintosh Human Interface Guidelines.*

For the classic book on usability testing, see Jakob Nielsen's *Usability Engineering.*

For details on both of these valuable resources, see "Related Books and Web Sites" on page xxii.

Graphic Conventions

Screen shots in this book illustrate the use of JFC components in applications with the Java look and feel. Because such applications typically run inside windows provided and managed by the native platform, the screen shots show assorted styles of windows and dialog boxes from the Microsoft Windows, Macintosh, and CDE (Common Desktop Environment) platforms.

Throughout the text, symbols are used to call your attention to design guidelines. Each type of guideline is identified by a unique symbol.

Java Look and Feel Standards

Requirements for the consistent appearance and compatible behavior of Java look and feel applications.

Java look and feel standards promote flexibility and ease of use in cross-platform applications and support the creation of applications that are accessible to all users, including users with physical and cognitive limitations. These standards require you to take actions that go beyond the provided appearance and behavior of the JFC components.

Occasionally, you might need to violate these standards. In such situations, use your discretion to balance competing requirements. Be sure to engage in user testing to validate your judgments.

Cross-Platform Delivery Guidelines   Recommendations for dealing with colors, fonts, keyboard operations, and other issues that arise when you want to deliver your application to a variety of computers running a range of operating systems.

Internationalization Guidelines   Advice for creating applications that can be adapted to the global marketplace.

Implementation Tips   Technical information and useful tips of particular interest to the programmers who are implementing your application design.

Related Books and Web Sites   Many excellent references are available on topics such as fundamental principles of human interface design, design issues for specific (or multiple) platforms, and issues relating to accessibility, internationalization, and applet design.

Design Principles   The resources in this section provide information on the fundamental concepts underlying human-computer interaction and interface design.

Baecker, Ronald M., William Buxton, and Jonathan Grudin, eds. *Readings in Human-Computer Interaction: Toward the Year 2000,* 2d ed. Morgan Kaufman, 1995. Based on research from graphic and industrial design and studies of cognition and group process, this volume addresses the efficiency and adequacy of human interfaces.

Hurlburt, Allen. *The Grid: A Modular System for the Design and Production of Newspapers, Magazines, and Books.* John Wiley & Sons, 1997. This is an excellent starting text. Although originally intended for print design, this book contains many guidelines that are applicable to software design.

IBM Human-Computer Interaction Group. "IBM Ease of Use." Available: `http://www.ibm.com/ibm/easy`. This web site covers many fundamental aspects of human interface design.

Laurel, Brenda, ed. *Art of Human-Computer Interface Design*. Addison-Wesley, 1990. Begun as a project inside Apple, this collection of essays explores the reasoning behind human-computer interaction and looks at the future of the relationship between humans and computers.

Mullet, Kevin, and Darrell Sano. *Designing Visual Interfaces: Communication Oriented Techniques.* Prentice Hall, 1995. This volume covers fundamental design principles, common mistakes, and step-by-step techniques for handling the visual aspects of interface design.

Nielsen, Jakob. *Usability Engineering.* AP Professional, 1994. This classic covers international user interfaces (including gestural interfaces), international usability engineering, guidelines for internationalization, resource separation, and interfaces for more than one locale.

Norman, Donald A. *The Design of Everyday Things.* Doubleday, 1990. A well-liked, amusing, and discerning examination of why some products satisfy while others only baffle or disappoint. Photographs and illustrations throughout complement the analysis of psychology and design.

Shneiderman, Ben. *Designing the User Interface: Strategies for Effective Human-Computer Interaction*, 3d ed. Addison-Wesley, 1997. The third edition of this best-seller adds new chapters on the World Wide Web, information visualization, and cooperative work and expands earlier work on development methodologies, evaluation techniques, and tools for building user interfaces.

Tognazzini, Bruce. *Tog On Interface.* Addison-Wesley, 1992. Based on a human interface column that Tognazzini wrote for Apple developers, this book delves into the pivotal challenges of user interface design, including the difficulties inherent in multimedia software.

Tufte, Edward R. *Envisioning Information.* Graphics Press, 1990. One of the best books on graphic design, this volume catalogues instances of superb information design (with an emphasis on maps and cartography) and analyzes the concepts behind their implementation.

Tufte, Edward R. *The Visual Display of Quantitative Information.* Graphics Press, 1992. Tufte explores the presentation of statistical information in charts and graphs with apt graphical examples and elegantly interwoven text.

Tufte, Edward R. *Visual Explanations: Images and Quantities, Evidence and Narrative.* Graphics Press, 1997. The third volume in Tufte's series on information display focuses on data that changes over time. Tufte explores the depiction of action and cause and effect through such examples as the explosion of the space shuttle Challenger, magic tricks, and a cholera epidemic in 19th-century London.

Design for Specific Platforms   The resources in this section cover application
design for the CDE, IBM, Java, Macintosh, and Microsoft Windows platforms.

CDE   Three volumes address the needs of designers and related professionals
creating applications using CDE and Motif 2.1.

The Open Group, 1997. *CDE 2.1/Motif 2.1–Style Guide and Glossary.*

The Open Group, 1997. *CDE 2.1/Motif 2.1–Style Guide Reference.*

The Open Group, 1997. *CDE 2.1/Motif 2.1–Style Guide Certification Check List.*

They can be ordered from the Open Group at
`http://www.opengroup.org/public/pubs/catalog/mo.htm`.

IBM   *Object-Oriented Interface Design: IBM Common User Access Guidelines.* Que
Corp, 1992. Available: `http://www.ibm.com/ibm/hci/guidelines/`
`design/ui_design.html`. This book is out of print but available from
most or all IBM branch offices. A small portion of the printed book is
intertwined with a modest amount of more current material at this IBM web
site.

Java   Campione, Mary, and Kathy Walrath. *The Java Tutorial: Object-Oriented
Programming for the Internet,* 2d ed. Addison-Wesley, 1998. Full of examples,
this task-oriented book introduces you to fundamental Java concepts and
applications. Walrath and Campione describe the Java language, applet
construction, and the fundamental Java classes and cover the use of multiple
threads and networking features.

Campione, Mary, et al. *The Java Tutorial Continued: The Rest of the JDK.*
Addison-Wesley, 1998. The experts describe features added to the original
core Java platform with many self-paced, hands-on examples. The book
focuses on Java 2 APIs but also contains the information you need to use the
JDK 1.1 versions of the APIs.

Chan, Patrick. *The Java Developer's Almanac, 1999.* Addison-Wesley, 1999.
Organized to increase programming performance and speed, this book
provides a quick but comprehensive reference to the Java™ 2 Platform,
Standard Edition, v. 1.2.

Eckstein, Robert, Mark Loy, and Dave Wood. *Java Swing.* O'Reilly &
Associates, 1998. An excellent introduction to the Swing components, this
book documents the Swing and Accessibility application programming
interfaces. An especially useful chapter explains how to create a custom look
and feel.

Geary, David M. *Graphic Java 2: Mastering the JFC*. Volume 2, *Swing*. Prentice Hall, 1998. This comprehensive volume describes the skills needed to build professional, cross-platform applications that take full advantage of the Java Foundation Classes. The volume includes chapters on drag and drop, graphics, colors and fonts, image manipulation, double buffering, sprite animation, and clipboard and data transfer.

Sun Microsystems, Inc. *Java 2 Platform API Specification*. Available: `http://java.sun.com/products/jdk/1.2/docs/api/ overview-summary.html`. This web site provides up-to-date technical documentation on the Java 2 API.

Sun Microsystems, Inc. *Java Look and Feel Design Guidelines*. Available: `http://java.sun.com/products/jlf`. This web site contains an HTML version of this book.

Sun Microsystems, Inc. *The Java Tutorial: A Practical Guide for Programmers*. Available: `http://java.sun.com/docs/books/tutorial/ index.html`. This web site is divided into four trails: a getting started trail for those new to the Java language; a trail introducing the Java language with sections on writing applets, the essential Java classes, creating a GUI, and custom networking; a specialized trail addressing such topics as internationalization, 2D graphics, and security; and a trail providing a comprehensive example.

Topley, Kim. *Core Java Foundation Classes*. Prentice Hall Computer Books, 1998. Topley explains how to build basic Swing applications, with an emphasis on layout managers and basic graphics programming. The book also describes the creation of multiple document interface (MDI) applications.

Walker, Will. "The Multiplexing Look and Feel." Available: `http://java.sun.com/products/jfc/tsc/archive/ archive.html`. This article describes a special look and feel that provides a way to extend the features of a Swing GUI without having to create a new look and feel design. Walker describes an example application that can simultaneously provide audio output, Braille output, and the standard visual output of ordinary Swing applications.

Macintosh Apple Computer, Inc. *Macintosh Human Interface Guidelines*. Addison-Wesley, 1992. This volume is the official word on Macintosh user interface principles. It includes a superb bibliography with titles on animation, cognitive psychology, color, environmental design, graphic and information design, human-computer design and interaction, language, accessibility, visual thinking, and internationalization.

Apple Computer, Inc. *Mac OS 8 Human Interface Guidelines.* Available:
`http://developer.apple.com/techpubs/mac/HIGOS8Guide/`
`thig-2.html`. This site offers a supplement to *Macintosh Human Interface
Guidelines.*

Microsoft Windows   *Windows Interface Guidelines for Software Design.* Microsoft Press,
1995. Available: `http://msdn.microsoft.com/library/`. The official
book on Microsoft interface design contains specifications and guidelines for
designers who would like to enhance the usability of their programs. These
guidelines are available in print, and a modest portion of them is on the
World Wide Web. You can download an addendum to the book from
`http://msdn.microsoft.com/developer/userexperience/`
`winuiguide.asp`.

Design for Multiple Platforms

The books in this section discuss the complex issues
that arise when designing software that runs on many platforms.

McFarland, Aland, and Tom Dayton (with others). *Design Guide for
Multiplatform Graphical User Interfaces* (LP-R13). Bellcore, 1995. (Available
only from Bellcore. Call 800-521-2673 from US & Canada, +1-908-699-5800
from elsewhere.) This is an object-oriented style guide with extensive
guidelines and a good explanation of object-oriented user interface style from
the user's perspective.

Marcus, Aaron, Nick Smilonich, and Lynne Thompson. *The Cross-GUI
Handbook: For Multiplatform User Interface Design.* Addison-Wesley, 1995.
This source describes the graphical user interfaces of Microsoft Windows and
Windows NT, OSF/Motif, NeXTSTEP, IBM OS/2, and Apple Macintosh. The text
includes design guidelines for portability and migration and
recommendations for handling contradictory or inadequate human interface
guidelines.

Design for Internationalization

The books in this section describe software design
for the global marketplace.

Fernandes, Tony. *Global Interface Design: A Guide to Designing International
User Interfaces.* AP Professional, 1995. Fernandes addresses developers of
Internet software designed for a global market. He explains cultural
differences, languages and their variations, taboos, aesthetics, ergonomic
standards, and other issues designers must research and understand.

Guide to Macintosh Software Localization. Addison-Wesley, 1992. A thorough
and thoughtful discussion of the internationalization and localization
processes that should prove helpful for developers on any platform.

Kano, Nadine. *Developing International Software for Windows 95 and Windows NT*. Microsoft Press, 1993. Kano targets Microsoft's guidelines for creating international software to an audience with knowledge of Microsoft Windows coding techniques and C++. The work contains information on punctuation, sort orders, locale-specific code-page data, DBCS/Unicode mapping tables, and multilingual API functions and structures.

Luong, Tuoc V., James S.H. Lok, and Kevin Driscoll. *Internationalization: Developing Software for Global Markets*. John Wiley & Sons, 1995. The Borland internationalization team describes its procedures and methods with a focus on testing and quality assurance for translated software. This hands-on guide tells how to produce software that runs anywhere in the world without requiring expensive recompiling of source code.

Nielsen, Jakob, and Elisa M. Del Galdo, eds. *International User Interfaces*. John Wiley & Sons, 1996. This book discusses what user interfaces can and must do to become commercially viable in the global marketplace. Contributors discuss issues such as international usability engineering, cultural models, multiple-language documents, and multilingual machine translation.

O'Donnell, Sandra Martin. *Programming for the World: A Guide to Internationalization*. Prentice Hall, 1994. This theoretical handbook explains how to modify computer systems to accommodate the needs of international users. O'Donnell describes many linguistic and cultural conventions used throughout the world and discusses how to design with the flexibility needed for the global marketplace.

Uren, Emmanuel, Robert Howard, and Tiziana Perinotti. S*oftware Internationalization and Localization: An Introduction*. Van Nostrand Reinhold, 1993. This guide to software adaptation encourages developers to aim at producing localized software with the same capabilities as the original software while meeting local requirements and conventions.

Design for Accessibility
These resources explore how to design software that supports all users, including those with physical and cognitive limitations.

Bergman, Eric, and Earl Johnson. "Towards Accessible Human Interaction." In *Advances in Human-Computer Interaction*, edited by Jakob Nielsen, vol. 5. Ablex Publishing, 1995. Available: http://www.sun.com/tech/access/updt.HCI.advance.html. This article discusses the relevance of accessibility to human interface designers and explores the process of designing for ranges of user capabilities. It provides design guidelines for accommodating physical disabilities such as repetitive strain injuries (RSI), low vision, blindness, and hearing impairment. It also contains an excellent list of additional sources on accessibility issues.

Schwerdtfeger, Richard S. *IBM Guidelines for Writing Accessible Applications Using 100% Pure Java*. IBM Corporation, 1998. Available: `http://www.austin.ibm.com/sns/access.html`. This web site presents principles of accessibility, a checklist for software accessibility, and a list of references and resources. In addition, it provides discussions of accessibility for the web and for Java applications.

Schwerdtfeger, Richard S. *Making the GUI Talk*. BYTE, 1991. Available: `ftp://ftp.software.ibm.com/sns/sr-os2/sr2doc/guitalk.txt`. This speech deals with off-screen model technology and GUI screen readers.

Sun Microsystems, Inc. *Accessibility Quick Reference Guide.* Available: `http://www.sun.com/tech/access/access.quick.ref.html`. This site defines accessibility, lists steps to check and double-check your product for accessibility, and offers tips for making applications more accessible.

Sun Microsystems, Inc. "Enabling Technologies." Available: `http://www.sun.com/access`. This web site includes a primer on the Java platform and accessibility and describes the support for assistive technologies now provided by the Swing components of the Java Foundation Classes.

Design for Applets   These books provide a range of information on designing applets.

Gulbransen, David, Kenrick Rawlings, and John December. *Creating Web Applets With Java*. Sams Publishing, 1996. An introduction to Java applets, this book addresses nonprogrammers who want to incorporate preprogrammed Java applets into web pages.

Hopson, K.C., Stephen E. Ingram, and Patrick Chan. *Designing Professional Java Applets*. Sams Publishing, 1996. An advanced reference to developing Java applets for business, science, and research.

PART I: OVERVIEW

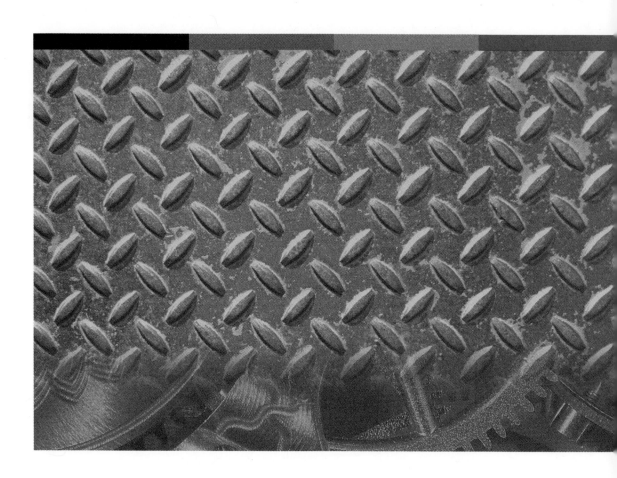

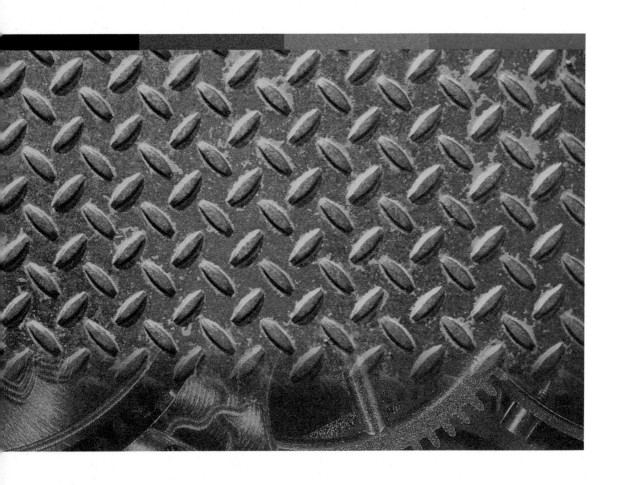

1: THE JAVA LOOK AND FEEL

As the Java platform has matured, designers and developers have recognized the need for consistent, compatible, and easy-to-use Java applications. The Java look and feel meets that need by providing a distinctive platform-independent appearance and standard behavior. The use of this single **look and feel** reduces design and development time and lowers training and documentation costs for all users.

This book sets standards for the use of the Java look and feel. By following these guidelines, you can create Java applications that effectively support all users worldwide, including those with physical and cognitive limitations.

Fundamentals of the Java Look and Feel

The Java look and feel is the default interface for applications built with the Java Foundation Classes. The Java look and feel is designed for cross-platform use and can provide:

- Consistency in the appearance and behavior of common design elements
- Compatibility with industry-standard components and interaction styles
- Aesthetic appeal that does not distract from application content

Three distinctive visual elements are the hallmarks of the Java look and feel components: the **flush 3D style**, the drag texture, and the color model.

In the Java look and feel, component surfaces appear to be at the same level as the surrounding canvas. This "flush 3D" style is illustrated in the following figure.

FIGURE 1   Consistent Use of the Flush 3D Style

The clean, modern appearance reduces the visual noise associated with beveled edges. Flush 3D components fit in with a variety of applications and operating systems.

A textured pattern, used throughout the Java look and feel, indicates items that users can drag. Such an indication cues cross-platform users in a reliable way. The following figure demonstrates several uses of the drag texture.

FIGURE 2   Consistent Use of the Drag Texture

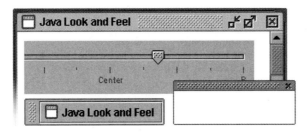

A simple and flexible color model ensures compatibility with platforms and devices capable of displaying quite different color depths. The default colors provide an aesthetically pleasing and comfortable scheme for interface elements, as shown in the following figure.

FIGURE 3   Role of the Color Model in Compatibility

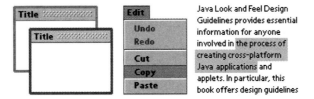

Visual Tour of the Java Look and Feel   The Java look and feel implements widely understood interface elements (windows, icons, menus, and pointers) and works in the same way on any operating system that supports the Java Foundation Classes (JFC). The visual tour in this section shows off two JFC applications with the Java look and feel: MetalEdit and Retirement Savings Calculator. MetalEdit is a standalone, text-editing application; Retirement Savings Calculator is an applet displayed in a browser window.

The following figure shows a Microsoft Windows desktop with MetalEdit and Retirement Savings Calculator. MetalEdit has a menu bar and toolbar as well as a text-editing area. Retirement Savings Calculator is displayed inside a web browser. Other Microsoft Windows applications are also present; some are represented by minimized windows.

Although the windows of many applications can be open on the desktop, only one can be the active window. In the figure, MetalEdit is the active window (indicated by the color of the title bar), whereas the Netscape Navigator™ browser, which contains Retirement Savings Calculator, is inactive. As an applet, Retirement Savings Calculator is displayed within an HTML page.

FIGURE 4   Typical Desktop With Applications on the Microsoft Windows Platform

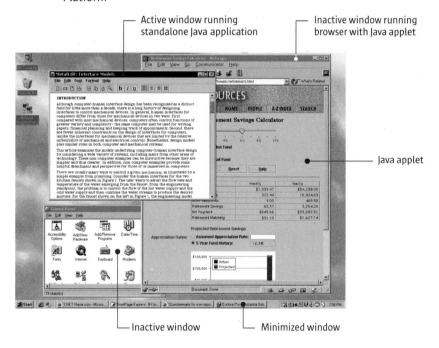

MetalEdit Application   This section uses a hypothetical text-editing application called "MetalEdit" to illustrate some of the most important visual characteristics of the Java look and feel, including its windows, menus, toolbars, editor panes, dialog boxes, and alert boxes.

Example Windows   The windows in Java look and feel applications use the borders, title bars, and window controls of the platform they are running on. For instance, the MetalEdit document window shown in Figure 4 on page 5 is running on a Microsoft Windows desktop and uses the standard Microsoft window frame and title bar. As shown in the following figure, the contents of the document window (menu bar, toolbar, and editor pane) use the Java look and feel. However, the window borders, title bars, and window controls have a platform-specific appearance.

FIGURE 5   Document Window on Three Platforms

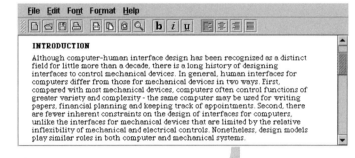

Java look and feel
window contents—
menu bar, toolbar,
and editor pane

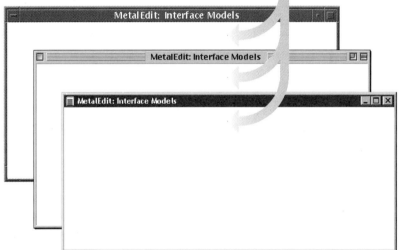

Platform-specific
borders, title bars,
and window
controls

Example Menus   The menu bar, which is the horizontal strip under the window title,
displays the titles of application menus, called "drop-down menus." Drop-
down menus provide access to an application's primary functions. They also
enable users to survey the features of the application by looking at the menu
items. Chapter 9 contains discussions of drop-down menus, submenus, and
contextual menus and provides guidelines for the creation of menus and
menu items for your application.

FIGURE 6   Example Menu Bar

The following figure shows the contents of the Edit and Format menus from the MetalEdit menu bar. The menu items are divided into logical groupings by menu separators (in the flush 3D style). For instance, in the Edit menu, the Cut, Copy, and Paste commands, which are related to the clipboard, are separated from Undo and Redo commands, which reverse or restore changes in the document. For more information, see "Separators" on page 136. Selected menu titles are highlighted in blue in the default Java look and feel theme. For details, see "Themes" on page 39.

FIGURE 7 Example Drop-down Menus

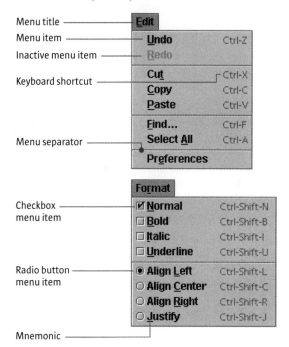

Keyboard shortcuts offer an alternative to using the mouse to choose a menu item. For instance, to copy a selection, users can press Control-C. For details, see "Keyboard Shortcuts" on page 87.

Mnemonics provide yet another way to access menu items. For instance, to view the contents of the Edit menu, users press Alt-E. Once the Edit menu has keyboard focus, users can press C to copy a selection. These alternatives are designated by underlining the "E" in Edit and the "C" in Copy. For details, see "Mnemonics" on page 88.

The menus shown in Figure 7 on page 7 illustrate two commonly used menu titles, menu items, and menu item arrangements for Java look and feel applications. For details, see "Drop-down Menus" on page 131 and "Menu Items" on page 132.

Example Toolbar   A toolbar displays command and toggle buttons that offer immediate access to the functions of many menu items. The MetalEdit toolbar is divided into four areas for functions relating to file management, editing, font styles, and alignment. Note the flush 3D style of the command and toggle buttons and the textured drag area to the left of the toolbar. For details, see "Toolbars" on page 140.

FIGURE 8   Example Toolbar

Drag area   Command buttons   Toggle buttons

Example Editor Pane   The document text in the following figure is displayed in an editor pane with a styled text editor plug-in kit, which is embedded in a scroll pane. (Note the use of the drag texture in the scroll box.) For more on styled text editor plug-in kits, see "Editor Panes" on page 170. For details on scroll panes, see "Scroll Panes" on page 102.

FIGURE 9   Example Editor Pane

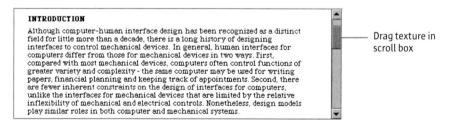

Drag texture in scroll box

Example Dialog Boxes   In the Java look and feel, dialog boxes use the borders and title bars of the platform they are running on. However, the dialog box contents have the Java look and feel. Chapter 8 describes dialog boxes in the Java look and feel and contains recommendations for their use.

Figure 10 on page 9 shows a preferences dialog box with the title bars, borders, and window controls of several platforms. The dialog box enables users to specify options in the MetalEdit application. Noneditable combo boxes are used to select ruler units and a font. Text fields are used to specify the margins. An editable combo box enables users to specify font size. Radio buttons and checkboxes are used to set other preferences. Clicking the Browse command button displays a file chooser in which users can select a stationery folder.

Note the flush 3D borders of the combo boxes, text fields, radio buttons, checkboxes, and command buttons. Labels use the primary 1 color, one of eight colors in the default Java look and feel theme. For a thorough treatment of basic controls (including combo boxes, radio buttons, checkboxes, and command buttons), see Chapter 10. For a detailed discussion of text fields and labels, see Chapter 11.

MetalEdit provides mnemonics and keyboard navigation and activation sequences for each of the interactive controls in the preferences dialog box. The dialog box in the following figure illustrates two ways to create a mnemonic: directly in a component, indicated by an underlined letter in the component text, or in a label associated with the component, indicated by an underlined letter in the label.

FIGURE 10   Example Dialog Boxes on Microsoft Windows, Macintosh, and CDE Platforms

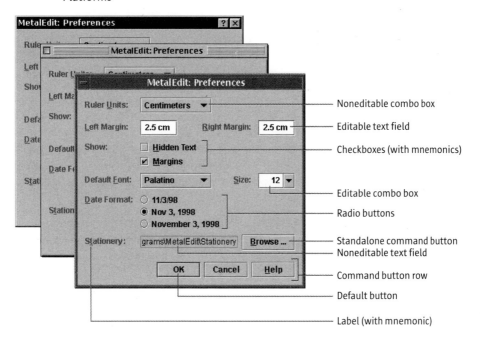

Example Alert Boxes   The alert boxes in a Java look and feel application use the borders, title bars, and window controls of the platform they are running on. However, the symbols, messages, and command buttons supplied by the JFC use the Java look and feel. (You provide the actual message and specify the number of command buttons as well as the button text. The JFC provides layouts for the symbol, the message, and the command buttons.)

When users try to close a window without saving changes, the Warning alert box asks them if they would like to save changes. Of the three command buttons in MetalEdit's Warning alert box, shown in the following figure, the default command button is Save. The Don't Save button closes the window without saving changes. The Cancel button closes the dialog box but leaves the unsaved document open. For details, see "Alert Boxes" on page 122.

FIGURE 11   Example Alert Boxes on CDE, Microsoft Windows, and Macintosh Platforms

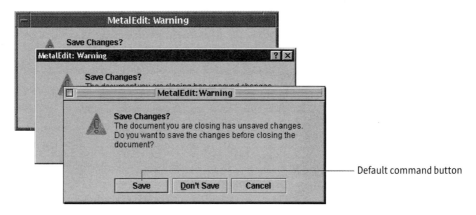

Retirement Savings Calculator Applet   The sample applet, Retirement Savings Calculator, is part of a web page displayed in the Netscape Navigator browser, as shown in the following figure. This human resources applet enables employees of a fictitious company to determine their contributions to a retirement savings plan. To make it easy for all employees to access information on their retirement savings, the company provides the applet in a web page. (Note the boundaries of the applet. The HTML page also includes a banner in the GIF format as well as an HTML header with the title of the page.) All the JFC components shown in the sample applet use the Java look and feel.

FIGURE 12   Applet on an HTML Page in a Browser (Exploded View)

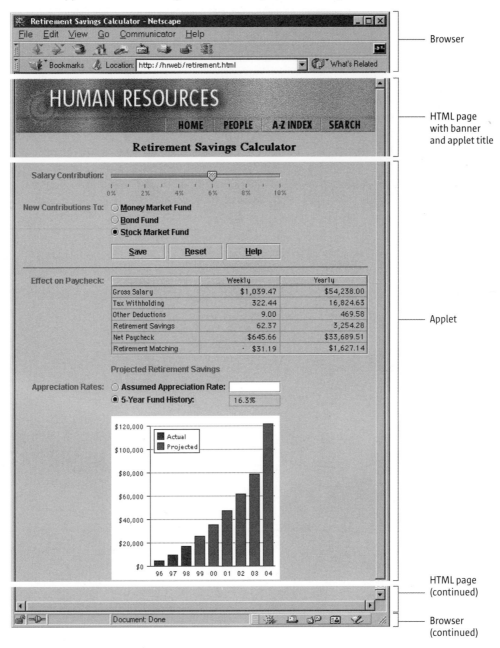

The applet obtains an employee's current retirement savings contribution and other salary data from a database and fills noneditable text fields with the relevant data. The employee can drag a slider to specify a salary contribution and click a radio button to specify whether new contributions go to a money market, bond, or stock market fund. A row of command buttons offers a choice of whether to save changes, reset the salary contribution, or display help.

Using the employee's input, the applet calculates the employee's weekly and yearly gross salary, tax withholding, other deductions, retirement savings contribution, net paycheck, and the company's matching funds. Results are displayed in a table. Finally, the employee can type an assumed appreciation rate in an editable text field to see accumulated future savings or instruct the applet to use the five-year fund history to project savings in the chart at the bottom of the applet.

FIGURE 13   Retirement Savings Calculator Applet

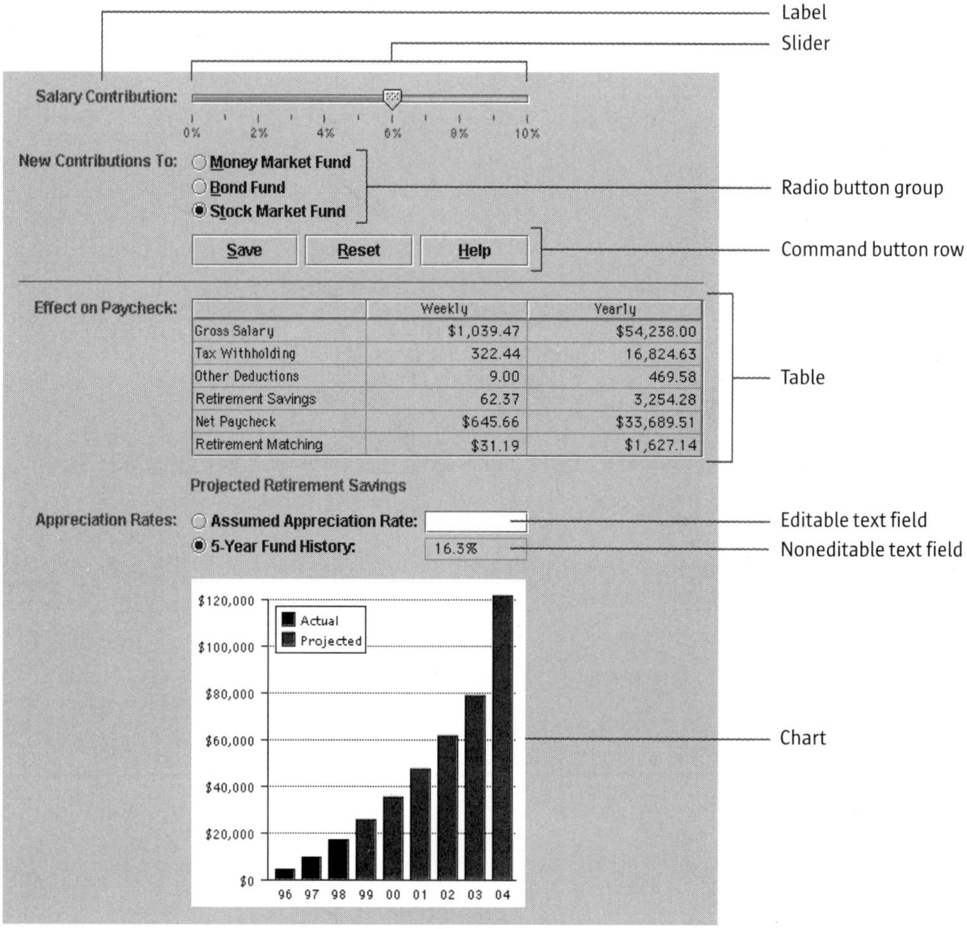

For more information on the components used in this applet, see "Text Fields" on page 167, "Sliders" on page 159, "Radio Buttons" on page 155, "Command Buttons" on page 148, and "Tables" on page 176.

2: THE JAVA FOUNDATION CLASSES

This book assumes that you are designing software based on the Java Foundation Classes and utilizing the Java look and feel. This chapter provides an overview of that technology: the Java Development Kit and Java™ 2 SDK, the user interface components of the Java Foundation Classes, the pluggable look and feel architecture, and available look and feel designs.

Java Development Kit

The APIs and tools that developers need to write, compile, debug, and run Java applications are included in the **Java Development Kit** (JDK™) and **Java 2 SDK**.

The guidelines in this book pertain to applications built with the Java 2 SDK, Standard Edition, v. 1.2 (referred to hereafter as "Java 2 SDK"), or the Java Development Kit versions 1.1.3 through 1.1.7 (referred to hereafter as "JDK 1.1"). The Java Foundation Classes are available for use with JDK 1.1, but they are an integral part of the Java 2 platform.

Java Foundation Classes

The **Java Foundation Classes** (JFC) include the **Swing classes**, which define a complete set of graphic interface components for JFC applications. An extension to the original Abstract Window Toolkit, the JFC includes the Swing classes, pluggable look and feel designs, and the Java Accessibility API, which are all implemented without **native code** (code that refers to the methods of a specific operating system or is compiled for a specific processor). The JFC components include windows and frames, panels and panes, dialog boxes, menus and toolbars, buttons, sliders, combo boxes, text components, tables, lists, and trees.

All the components have look and feel designs that you can specify. The cross-platform, default look and feel is the **Java look and feel**. For details on the design principles and visual elements underlying the Java look and feel, see Chapter 1.

▦⊃   In code, the Java look and feel is referred to as "Metal."

JDK 1.1 and the Java 2 SDK   The following figure summarizes the differences in the Java Foundation Classes in JDK 1.1 and the Java 2 SDK. Both development kits contain the **Abstract Window Toolkit** (AWT), the class library that provides the standard application programming interfaces for building graphical user interfaces for Java programs. There is native code in the AWT code in both kits, and in drag and drop and the Java 2D™ API in the Java 2 SDK.

FIGURE 14   Java Foundation Classes for JDK 1.1 and the Java 2 SDK

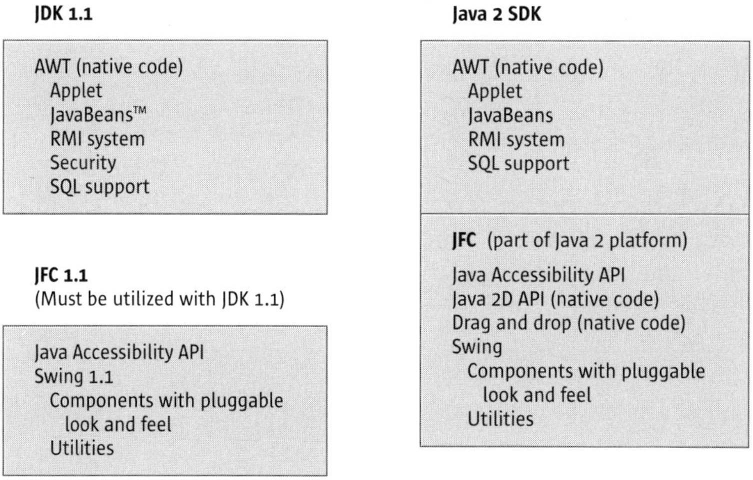

JDK 1.1

AWT (native code)
  Applet
  JavaBeans™
  RMI system
  Security
  SQL support

JFC 1.1
(Must be utilized with JDK 1.1)

Java Accessibility API
Swing 1.1
  Components with pluggable
    look and feel
  Utilities

Java 2 SDK

AWT (native code)
  Applet
  JavaBeans
  RMI system
  SQL support

JFC (part of Java 2 platform)

Java Accessibility API
Java 2D API (native code)
Drag and drop (native code)
Swing
  Components with pluggable
    look and feel
  Utilities

In the Java 2 SDK, the Java Foundation Classes also include the Java 2D API, drag and drop, and other enhancements. The **Java 2D API** provides an advanced two-dimensional imaging model for complex shapes, text, and images. Features include enhanced font and color support and a single, comprehensive rendering model.

Support for Accessibility   Three features of JDK 1.1 and the Java 2 SDK support people with special needs: the Java Accessibility API, the pluggable look and feel architecture, and keyboard navigation.

The **Java Accessibility API** provides ways for an assistive technology to interact and communicate with JFC components. A Java application that fully supports the Java Accessibility API is compatible with technologies such as screen readers and screen magnifiers. A separate package, **Java Accessibility Utilities**, provides support in locating the objects that implement the Java Accessibility API.

A pluggable look and feel architecture is used to build both visual and nonvisual designs, such as audio and tactile user interfaces. For more on the pluggable look and feel, see "Pluggable Look and Feel Architecture" on page 17.

Keyboard navigation enables users to move between components, open menus, highlight text, and so on. This support makes an application accessible to people who do not use a mouse. For details on keyboard operations, see Appendix A.

Support for Internationalization   JDK 1.1 and the Java 2 SDK provide internationalized text handling. This feature includes support for the bidirectional display of text lines—important for displaying documents that mix languages with a left-to-right text direction (for instance, English, German, or Japanese) and languages with a right-to-left direction (for instance, Arabic or Hebrew). JDK 1.1 and the Java 2 SDK also provide resource bundles, locale-sensitive sorting, and support for localized numbers, dates, times, and messages.

User Interface Components of the Java Foundation Classes

The Java Foundation Classes include Swing, a complete set of user interface components, including windows, dialog boxes, alert boxes, panels and panes, and basic controls. Each JFC component contains a model (the data structure) and a user interface (the presentation and behavior of the component), as shown in the following illustration.

FIGURE 15   Structure of the JFC Components

Model	User Interface

Pluggable Look and Feel Architecture   Because both presentation and behavior are separate and replaceable ("pluggable"), you can specify any of several look and feel designs for your application—or you can create your own look and feel. The separation of a component's model (data structure) from its user interface (display and interaction behavior) is the empowering principle behind the **pluggable look and feel architecture** of the JFC. A single **JFC application** can present a Java look and feel, a platform-specific look and feel, or a customized interface (for example, an audio interface).

Example Model and Interface   Consider the slider in the following figure as a simplified example. The slider's model contains information about the slider's current value, the minimum and maximum values, and other properties. The slider's user interface determines how users see or interact with the slider. The model knows almost nothing about the user interface—while the user interface knows a great deal about the model.

FIGURE 16   Pluggable Look and Feel Architecture of a Slider

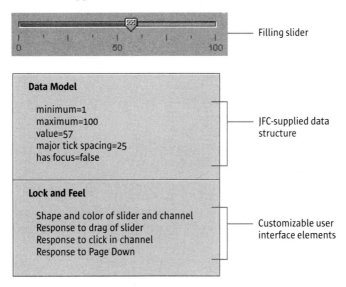

Filling slider

Data Model

minimum=1
maximum=100
value=57
major tick spacing=25
has focus=false

JFC-supplied data structure

Lock and Feel

Shape and color of slider and channel
Response to drag of slider
Response to click in channel
Response to Page Down

Customizable user interface elements

Client Properties   You can use the client properties mechanism to display an alternate form of a specific Java user interface component. If a look and feel design does not support the property, it ignores the property and displays the component as usual. You can set alternate appearances for sliders, toolbars, trees, and internal frames. For instance, a nonfilling slider is displayed by default. However, by using the client properties mechanism, you can display a filling slider, as shown in Figure 16 on page 18.

Major JFC User Interface Components   The following table illustrates the major user interface components in the JFC. Components are listed alphabetically by their names in code. Their English names are provided, followed by the location of more detailed information on each component.

TABLE 1   Names and Appearance of the JFC User Interface Components

Component	Code Name	Common Name	For Details
	JApplet	Applet	page 27
	JButton	Command button and toolbar button	page 148 and page 142
	JCheckBox	Checkbox	page 154
	JCheckBoxMenuItem	Checkbox menu item	page 135
	JColorChooser	Color chooser	page 126
	JComboBox	Noneditable and editable combo boxes	page 156
	JDesktopPane	Desktop pane	page 108
	JDialog	Dialog box, secondary window, and utility window	page 111, page 98, and page 100
	JEditorPane	Editor pane	page 170

TABLE 1   Names and Appearance of the JFC User Interface Components *(Continued)*

Component	Code Name	Common Name	For Details
	JFrame	Primary window	page 95
	JInternalFrame	Internal frame, minimized internal frame, and palette window	page 108, page 109, and page 110
label	JLabel	Label	page 164
	JList	List	page 173
	JMenu	Drop-down menu and submenu	page 131 and page 132
File	JMenuBar	Menu bar	page 130
	JMenuItem	Menu item	page 132
	JOptionPane	Alert box	page 122
	JPanel	Panel	page 101
###	JPasswordField	Password field	page 168

TABLE 1   Names and Appearance of the JFC User Interface Components *(Continued)*

Component	Code Name	Common Name	For Details
	JPopupMenu	Contextual menu	page 139
	JProgressBar	Progress bar	page 160
	JRadioButton	Radio button	page 155
	JRadioButtonMenuItem	Radio button menu item	page 135
	JScrollBar	Scrollbar	page 102
	JScrollPane	Scroll pane	page 102
	JSeparator	Separator	page 136
	JSlider	Slider	page 159
	JSplitPane	Split pane	page 106
	JTabbedPane	Tabbed pane	page 104

TABLE 1   Names and Appearance of the JFC User Interface Components *(Continued)*

Component	Code Name	Common Name	For Details
	`JTable`	Table	page 176
	`JTextArea`	Plain text area	page 169
	`JTextField`	Noneditable and editable text fields (single line)	page 167
	`JTextPane`	Editor pane with the styled editor kit plug-in	page 170
	`JToggleButton`	Toggle button and toolbar button	page 152 and page 142
	`JToolBar`	Toolbar	page 140
	`JToolTip`	Tool tip	page 145
	`JTree`	Tree view	page 187
	`JWindow`	Plain (unadorned) window	page 99

In the JFC, the typical primary windows that users work with are based on the `JFrame` component. Unadorned windows that consist of a rectangular region without any title bar, close control, or other window controls are based on the `JWindow` component. Designers and developers typically use the `JWindow` component to create windows without title bars, such as splash screens.

For details on the use of windows, frames, panels, and panes, see Chapter 7.

Look and Feel Options

You, the designer, have the first choice of a look and feel design. You can determine the look and feel you want users to receive on a specific platform, or you can choose a **cross-platform** look and feel.

Java Look and Feel—the Recommended Design

With a cross-platform look and feel, your application will appear and perform the same everywhere, simplifying the application's development and documentation.

☕ Specify the Java look and feel, which is a cross-platform look and feel, explicitly. If you do not specify a look and feel or if an error occurs while specifying the name of a look and feel, the Java look and feel is used by default.

▤▷ The following code can be used to specify the Java look and feel explicitly:

```
UIManager.setLookAndFeel(
UIManager.getCrossPlatformLookAndFeelClassName() );
```

Alternative Approaches

If you do not specify the Java look and feel, you can specify:

- A particular look and feel—one that ships with the JFC or one that someone else has made. Note, however, that not all look and feel designs are available on every platform. For example, the Microsoft Windows look and feel is available only on the Microsoft Windows platform.

- An auxiliary look and feel—one that is designed to be used in addition to the primary look and feel. By combining look and feel designs, you can target different ways of perceiving information.

Because there is far more to the design of an application than the look and feel of components, it is unwise to give end users the ability to swap look and feel designs while working in your application. Switching look and feel designs in this way only swaps the look and feel designs of the components from one platform to another. The layout and vocabulary used are platform-specific and do not change. For instance, swapping look and feel designs does not change the titles of the menus.

☕ Make it possible for your users to specify an auxiliary look and feel design, which provides alternative methods of information input and output for people with special needs.

Supplied Designs   The look and feel designs available in JDK 1.1 and the Java 2 SDK
are:

- **Java look and feel.** (Called "Metal" in the code.) The Java look and feel is
  designed for use on any platform that supports the JFC. This book
  provides recommendations on the use of the Java look and feel.

- **Microsoft Windows.** (Called "Windows" in the code.) The Microsoft
  Windows style look and feel can be used only on Microsoft Windows
  platforms. It follows the behavior of the components in applications that
  ship with Windows NT 4.0. For details, see *Windows Interface Guidelines
  for Software Design*.

- **CDE.** (Called "CDE/Motif" in the code.) The CDE style look and feel is
  designed for use on UNIX® platforms. It emulates OSF/Motif 1.2.5, which
  ships with the Solaris™ 2.6 operating system. It can run on any platform.
  For details, see the *CDE 2.1/Motif 2.1 — Style Guide and Glossary*.

In addition, you can download the Macintosh style look and feel (called "Mac
OS" in the code) separately. The Macintosh style look and feel can be used
only on Macintosh operating systems. It follows the specification for
components under Mac OS 8.1. For details, see the *Mac OS 8 Human
Interface Guidelines*.

PART II: FUNDAMENTAL JAVA APPLICATION DESIGN

3: DESIGN CONSIDERATIONS

When you begin a software project, ask yourself these three questions:

- How do I want to deliver my software to users?
- How can I design an application that is accessible to all potential users?
- How can I design an application that suits a global audience and requires minimal effort to localize?

Choosing an Application or an Applet

At the beginning of the development process, you must decide if you want to create a standalone **application** or an **applet** that is displayed in a web **browser**. The following figure shows the different environments for running applications and applets.

FIGURE 17   Environments for Applications and Applets

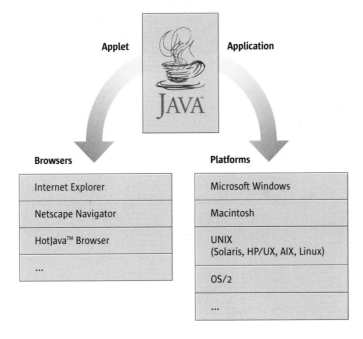

When deciding between an application and an applet, the two main issues you need to consider are distribution and security, including read and write permissions. If you decide to use an applet, you must also decide whether to display your applet in the user's current browser window or in a separate browser window.

For an example of an application that uses the Java look and feel, see "MetalEdit Application" on page 5. For an example of an applet, see "Retirement Savings Calculator Applet" on page 10. For a list of additional reading on applets, see "Design for Applets" on page xxviii.

Distribution   When deciding how to distribute your software, weigh the needs of both end users and administrators. Don't forget to consider ease-of-use issues for:

- Initial distribution and installation of the software
- Maintenance of the software
- Updates to the software
- Daily access to the software

At one extreme is the standalone application, distributed on a CD-ROM disc or a floppy disk and installed on the end user's local hard disk. Once the application is installed, users can easily access it. In an enterprise environment, however, maintenance can be complicated because separate copies of the application exist on each user's local computer. Distribution of the original application and subsequent updates require shipment of the software to, and installation by, multiple users.

In contrast, applets are simpler to distribute and maintain because they are installed on a central web server. Using a web browser on their local machines, users can access the latest version of the applet from anywhere on the intranet or Internet. Users, however, must download the applet over the network each time they start the applet.

If you are creating an applet, make sure that your users have a browser that contains the JFC or that they are using Java™ Plug-In. That way, users will not have to download the JFC every time they run the applet.

Security Issues   Another issue to consider is whether your software needs to read and write files. Standalone Java applications can read or write files on the user's hard disk just as other applications do. For example, the MetalEdit application reads and writes documents on the user's local disk.

In contrast, applets usually cannot access a user's hard disk because they are intended for display on a web page, which might come from an unknown source. Applets are better suited for tasks that do not require access to a user's hard disk. For example, a web page for a bank might offer an applet that calculates home mortgage payments and prints results, but does not save files on the customer's hard disk.

You can also use applets as a front end to a central database. For example, the Retirement Savings Calculator applet enables company employees to select funds for their retirement contribution and update the amount of their contribution in the company database.

Placement of Applets   If you decide to design an applet, you can display your applet in the user's current browser window or in a separate browser window.

Applets in the User's Current Browser Window   The current browser window is well suited for displaying applets in which users perform a single task. This approach enables users to perform the task and then resume other activities in the browser, such as surfing the web.

An applet displayed in the current browser window should not include a menu bar—having a menu bar in both the applet and the browser might confuse users. The mnemonics assigned in the applet must also be different from the mnemonics used to control the browser window; otherwise, the mnemonics might conflict.

A disadvantage of using the current browser window is that the applet terminates when users navigate to another web page. The current settings and data in the applet are lost. To use the applet again, users must navigate back to the page that contains the applet and reload the page.

Applets in Separate Browser Windows   If your applet involves more than one task or if users might visit other web pages before completing the task, launch a separate browser window and display the applet there. This approach enables users to interact with the applet and maintain the original browser window for other activities. Navigating to another web page in the original browser window does not affect the applet in the separate browser window.

Designing an applet for a separate browser window is simpler if you remove the browser's normal menu and navigation controls. Doing so avoids confusion between the browser's menu and controls and the applet's menus and controls. You also avoid potential conflicts between mnemonics in the two windows.

Designing for Accessibility

Accessibility refers to the removal of barriers that prevent people with disabilities from participating in social, professional, and practical life activities. In software design, **accessibility** requires taking into account the needs of people with functional differences: for example, users who are unable to operate a conventional mouse or keyboard or users who cannot process information using traditional output methods.

Benefits of Accessibility

Providing computer access to users with disabilities offers social, economic, and legal benefits. Accessible software increases the opportunities for employment, independence, and productivity for the approximately 750 million people worldwide with disabilities.

Building accessibility into an application makes it easier to use for a wide range of people, not only those with disabilities. For example, mnemonics, which provide an alternate keyboard method for accomplishing tasks in an application, aid users with physical disabilities as well as blind and low-vision users. Mnemonics are also broadly employed by "power" users.

Many countries are instituting legislation that makes access to information, products, and services mandatory for individuals with special needs. In these countries, government and academic institutions are required to purchase and support technologies that maximize accessibility. For example, in the United States, Section 508 of the Federal Rehabilitation Act requires all federal contracts to include solutions for employees with disabilities. The international community of people with disabilities is also successfully pressuring companies to sell accessible software.

Accessible Design

Five steps will put you on a path to an accessible product:

- Follow the standards in this book
- Provide accessible names and descriptions for your components
- Employ mnemonics and keyboard shortcuts throughout your application
- Provide proper keyboard navigation and activation
- Perform usability tests

For a list of additional reading, see "Design for Accessibility" on page xxvii.

Java Look and Feel Standards   The Java look and feel standards in this book take into account the needs of users with functional limitations. The standards cover how to use colors, fonts, animation, and graphics. By following these standards, you will be able to meet the needs of most of your users.

☕ Java look and feel standards are identified throughout the book by this symbol.

Accessible Names and Descriptions   You should provide an accessible name and description for each component in your application. These properties enable an **assistive technology**, such as a screen reader, to interact with the component.

⊟▭ The accessibleName property provides a name for a component and distinguishes it from other components of the same type.

⊟▭ The accessibleDescription property provides additional information about a component, such as how it works. Setting a component's accessibleDescription property is equivalent to providing a tool tip for the component.

⊟▭ The Ferret utility tool can be used to check that an accessibleName and other API information are properly implemented in your application. Ferret is part of the Java Accessibility Utilities package.

For more information on the Java Accessibility API and the Java Accessibility Utilities package, see "Support for Accessibility" on page 16.

Mnemonics   You should provide mnemonics throughout your application. A mnemonic is an underlined letter that shows users which key to press (in conjunction with the Alt key) to activate a command or navigate to a component. The following dialog box shows the use of mnemonics for a text field, checkboxes, radio buttons, and command buttons. For example, if keyboard focus is within the dialog box, pressing Alt-W moves keyboard focus to the Whole Word checkbox.

FIGURE 18   Mnemonics in a Dialog Box

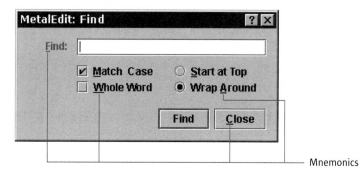

In cases where you can't add a mnemonic to the component itself, as in the text field in the preceding figure, you can place the mnemonic in the component's label. For more information on mnemonics, see "Mnemonics" on page 88.

⊞⇨ The labelFor property can be used to associate a label with another component so that the component becomes active when the label's mnemonic is activated.

Keyboard Focus and Tab Traversal   You can also assist users who navigate via the keyboard by assigning initial keyboard focus and by specifying a tab traversal order. Keyboard focus indicates where the next keystrokes will take effect. For more information, see "Keyboard Focus" on page 83.

Tab traversal order is the sequence in which components receive keyboard focus on successive presses of the Tab key. In most cases, the traversal order follows the reading order of the users' locale. For more information on tab traversal order, see "Tab Traversal Order" on page 114.

Make sure you test your application to see if users can access all functions and interactive components from the keyboard. Unplug the mouse and use only the keyboard when you perform your test.

Usability Testing   You should test the application with a variety of users to see how well it provides for accessibility. Low-vision users, for example, are sensitive to font sizes and color, as well as layout and context problems. Blind users are affected by interface flow, tab order, layout, and terminology. Users with mobility impairments can be sensitive to tasks that require an excessive number of steps or a wide range of movement.

Planning for Internationalization and Localization

In software development, **internationalization** is the process of writing an application that is suitable for the global marketplace, taking into account variations in regions, languages, and cultures. A related term, **localization**, refers to the process of customizing an application for a particular language or region. The language, meaning, or format of the following types of data can vary with locale:

- Colors
- Currency formats
- Date and time formats
- Graphics
- Icons
- Labels
- Messages
- Number formats
- Online help
- Page layouts
- Personal titles
- Phone numbers
- Postal addresses
- Sounds
- Units of measurement

The following figure shows a notification dialog box in both English and Japanese. Much of the localization of this dialog box involves the translation of text. The Japanese dialog box is bigger than the English dialog box because some text strings are longer. Note the differences in the way that mnemonics are displayed. In English, the mnemonic for the Sound File text field is <u>S</u>. In Japanese, the same mnemonic (<u>S</u>) is placed at the end of the label.

FIGURE 19   English and Japanese Notification Dialog Boxes

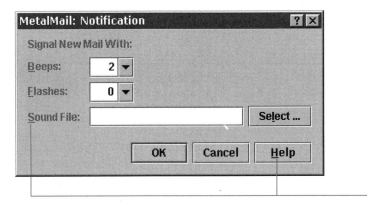

Mnemonics

Mnemonics

Benefits of Global Planning   The main benefit of designing an application for the global marketplace is more customers. Many countries require that companies purchase applications that support their language and culture. Global planning ensures that your application is easier to translate and maintain (because it has a single source file). A well-designed application will function the same way in all locales.

Global Design   You can incorporate support for localization into your design by using JFC-supplied layout managers and resource bundles. In addition, you should take into account that differences exist around the world in reading order, text, mnemonics, graphics, formats, sorting orders, and fonts.

⊕ Internationalization guidelines are identified throughout the book by this symbol. For a list of additional reading, see "Design for Internationalization" on page xxvi.

Layout Managers   You can use a **layout manager** to control the size and location of the components in your application. For example, Figure 19 on page 34 shows that the Sound File label becomes longer when it is translated from English to Japanese. The spacing between the Sound File label and its text field, however, is the same in both dialog boxes. For more information on layout managers, see *The Java Tutorial* at
`http://java.sun.com/docs/books/tutorial`.

Resource Bundles   You should use resource bundles to store locale-specific data, such as text, colors, graphics, fonts, and mnemonics. A **resource bundle** makes your application easier to localize because it provides locale-specific data without changing the application source code. If your application has a Cancel button, for example, the resource bundles in English, German, and Japanese would include the text shown in the following figure.

FIGURE 20   Cancel Buttons in English, German, and Japanese

For more information on creating resource bundles, see *The Java Tutorial*.

Reading Order   When you lay out your application, place the components according to your users' reading order. This order will help users understand the components quickly as they read through them. Reading orders vary among locales. The reading order in English, for example, is left to right and top to bottom. The reading order in Middle Eastern languages, on the other hand, is from right to left and top to bottom.

In this book, you will find standards such as "put labels before the component they describe." The term "before" is determined by the reading order of the user's language. For example, in English, labels appear to the left of the component they describe.

⊟▷ In the Java 2 SDK, the layout managers `FlowLayout` and `BorderLayout` are sensitive to the reading order of the locale.

Word Order   Keep in mind that word order varies among languages, as shown in the following figure. A noneditable combo box that appears in the middle of an English sentence does not translate properly in French, where the adjective should come after the noun. (The correct French sentence is "Utilisez une Flèche Rouge.")

FIGURE 21   Correct Word Order in English But Not in French

The following figure corrects the problem by using a label before the noneditable combo box. This format works well in both English and French.

FIGURE 22   Correct Word Order in Both English and French

Mnemonics   You must be careful when choosing mnemonics, which might change in different languages. Make sure that the characters you choose for your mnemonics are available on international keyboards. In addition, store mnemonics in resource bundles with the rest of the application's text.

Graphics   You can make localization easier by using globally understood graphics whenever possible. Many graphics that are easily understood in one locale are puzzling in another locale. For example, using a mailbox to represent an email application is problematic because the shape and size of mailboxes vary by locale. Graphics that represent everyday objects, holidays, and seasons are difficult to localize, as are graphics that include text.

Avoid using graphics that might be offensive in some locales. For example, many hand positions are considered obscene gestures. Other graphics that sometimes cause offense are pictures of animals and people. An example of a symbol that works well in all cultures is the use of an airplane to denote an airport.

Like text, you can place graphics in resource bundles so that the translators can change them without changing the application source code. The ability to change graphics also benefits users with visual impairments.

Formats   You can use the formatting classes provided in the Java 2 SDK to automatically format numbers, currencies, dates, and times for a specific locale. For example, in English, a date might appear as July 26, 1987, and the time as 3:17 p.m. In German, the same date is written as 26 Juli 1987 and the time is 15:17 Uhr.

⊞▭   For numbers and currencies, the class is `NumberFormat`; for dates and times, the class is `DateFormat`; and for strings that contain variable data, the class is `MessageFormat`. The formatting classes are part of the `java.text` package.

Sort Order   You can use the collator classes provided in the Java 2 SDK to enable the sorting of strings by locale. For example, in Roman languages, sorting is commonly based on alphabetical order (which might vary from one language to another). In other languages, sorting might be based on phonetics, character radicals, the number of character strokes, and so on.

⊞▭   The `Collator` class in the `java.text` package enables locale-sensitive string sorting.

Fonts   You can place fonts in resource bundles so that they can be changed by the localizers. The ability to change fonts also benefits users with visual impairments who read print with a magnifier or screen reader.

Usability Testing   Two tests done early in the design process can show you how well your application works in the global marketplace. First, you can send draft designs of your application to your translators. Second, you can test your application with users from the locales you are targeting (for example, test a Japanese version of the application with Japanese users). This test will help you to determine whether users understand how to use the product, if they perceive the graphics and colors as you intended them, and if there is anything offensive in the product.

4: VISUAL DESIGN

Visual design and aesthetics affect user confidence in and comfort with your application. A polished and professional look without excess or oversimplification is not easy to attain. This chapter discusses these high-level, visual aspects of Java look and feel applications:

- Use of themes to control and change the colors and fonts of components to suit your requirements

- Capitalization of text in interface elements to ensure consistency and readability

- Layout and alignment of interface elements to enhance clarity, ease of use, and aesthetic appeal

- Use of animation to provide progress and status feedback

Themes

You can use the **theme mechanism** to control many of the fundamental attributes of the Java look and feel design, including colors and fonts. You might want to change the colors to match your corporate identity, or you might increase color contrast and font size to enable users with visual impairments to use your application. The theme mechanism enables you to specify alternative colors and fonts across an entire Java look and feel application.

The technical documentation for the class `javax.swing.plaf.metal.DefaultMetalTheme` is available at the Swing Connection web site at `http://java.sun.com/products/jfc/tsc`.

Colors   If you want to change the color theme of your application, be sure that your interface elements remain visually coherent. The Java look and feel uses a simple color model so that it can run on a variety of platforms and on devices capable of displaying various depths of color. Eight colors are defined for the interface:

- Three primary colors to give the theme a color identity and to emphasize selected items

- Three secondary colors, typically shades of gray, for neutral drawing and inactive items

- Two additional colors, usually defined as black and white, for the display of text and highlights

Within the primary and secondary color groups in the default theme, there is a gradation from dark (primary 1 and secondary 1) to lighter (primary 2 and secondary 2) to lightest (primary 3 and secondary 3).

Primary Colors   The visual elements of Java look and feel applications use the primary colors as follows:

- Primary 1 for active window borders, shadows of selected items, and labels

- Primary 2 for selected menu titles and items, active scroll boxes, and progress bar fill

- Primary 3 for large colored areas, such as the title bar of active internal frames and selected text

The usage is illustrated in the following figure.

FIGURE 23   Primary Colors in Default Color Theme

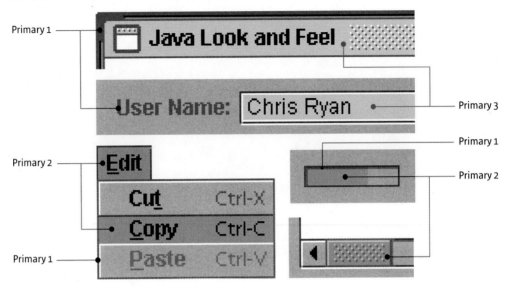

Secondary Colors   The visual elements of Java look and feel applications use the secondary colors as follows:

- Secondary 1 for the dark border that creates flush 3D effects for items such as command buttons

- Secondary 2 for inactive window borders, shadows, pressed buttons, and dimmed command button text

- Secondary 3 for the background canvas and inactive title bars for internal frames

The usage is shown in the following figure.

FIGURE 24   Secondary Colors in Default Color Theme

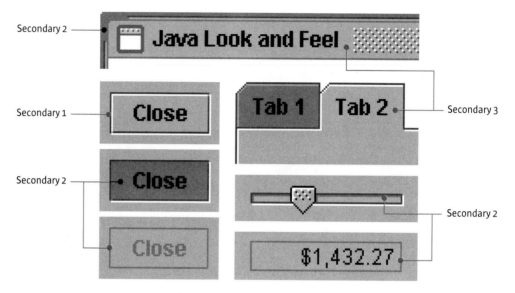

Black and White   Black and white have defined roles in the Java look and feel color model. In particular, black appears in:

- User text, such as the entry in an editable text field

- Control text, such as menu titles and menu items

- Title text in the internal frame as well as the button text in command buttons

- Tab text in tabbed panes

- Text in noneditable text fields

White is used for:

- Highlighting the flush 3D appearance of such components as command buttons

- Highlighting in menus

Default Java Look and Feel Theme   The following table summarizes the eight colors defined in the Java look and feel. It provides swatches and values representing each color in the default theme. It also gives details about the roles each color plays in basic drawing, three-dimensional effects, and text.

TABLE 2   Colors of the Default Java Look and Feel Theme

	Name	Basic Drawing	3D Effects	Text
⬛	Primary 1 RGB 102-102-153 Hex #666699	Active window borders	Shadows of selected items	System text (for example, labels)
⬛	Primary 2 RGB 153-153-204 Hex #9999CC	Highlighting and selection (for example, of menu titles and menu items); indication of keyboard focus	Shadows (color)	
⬜	Primary 3 RGB 204-204-255 Hex #CCCCFF	Large colored areas (for example, the active title bar)		Text selection
⬛	Secondary 1 RGB 102-102-102 Hex #666666		Dark border for flush 3D style	
⬛	Secondary 2 RGB 153-153-153 Hex #999999	Inactive window borders	Shadows; button mousedown	Dimmed text (for example, inactive menu items or labels)
⬜	Secondary 3 RGB 204-204-204 Hex #CCCCCC	Canvas color (that is, normal background color); inactive title bar		
⬛	Black RGB 000-000-000 Hex #000000			User text and control text (including items such as menu titles)
⬜	White RGB 255-255-255 Hex #FFFFFF		Highlights	Background for user text entry area

☕ Unless you are defining a reverse-video theme, maintain a dark-to-light gradation like the one in the default theme so that interface objects are properly rendered. To reproduce three-dimensional effects correctly, make your secondary 1 color darker than secondary 3 (the background color); make secondary 2 (used for highlights) lighter than the background color.

☕ Ensure that primary 1 (used for labels) has enough contrast with the background color (secondary 3) to make text labels easily readable.

Redefinition of Colors   The simplest modification you can make to the color theme is to redefine the primary colors. For instance, you can substitute greens for the purple-blues used in the default theme, as shown in the following figure.

FIGURE 25   Green Color Theme

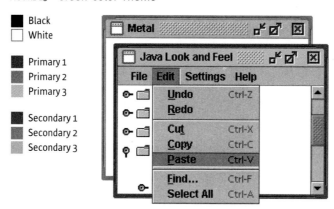

You can use the same value for more than one of the eight colors—for instance, a high-contrast theme might use only black, white, and grays. The following figure shows a theme that uses the same grays for primary 2 and secondary 2. White functions as primary 3 and secondary 3 as well as in its normal role.

FIGURE 26   High-Contrast Color Theme

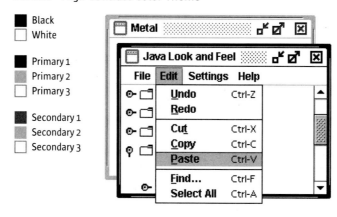

Fonts   As part of the theme mechanism and parallel to the color model, the Java look and feel provides a default font style model for a consistent look. You can use themes to redefine font typefaces, sizes, and styles in your application. The default Java look and feel theme defines four type styles: the control font, the system font, the user font, and the small font. The actual fonts used vary across platforms.

The following table shows the mappings to Java look and feel components for the default theme.

TABLE 3   Type Styles Defined by the Java Look and Feel

Type Style	Default Theme	Uses
Control	12-point bold	Buttons, checkboxes, menu titles, and window titles
Small	10-point plain	Keyboard shortcuts in menus and tool tips
System	12-point plain	Tree views and tool tips
User	12-point plain	Text fields and tables

To ensure consistency, ease of use, and visual appeal, use the supplied default fonts unless there is compelling reason for an application-wide change (such as higher readability). Use the theme mechanism if you do make modifications.

Do not write font sizes or styles directly into your application source code. Some users might be able to read print only with a screen reader or a magnifier.

Use the appropriate layout manager to ensure that the layout of your application can handle different font sizes.

Ensure that the font settings you choose are legible and can be rendered well on your target systems.

In the default theme, six methods are used to return references to the four type styles. The getControlTextFont, getMenuTextFont, and getWindowTitleFont methods return the control font; getSystemTextFont returns the system font; getUserTextFont returns the user font; and getSubTextFont returns the small font.

All fonts in the Java look and feel are defined in the default Java look and feel theme as Dialog, which maps to a platform-specific font.

Capitalization of Text in the Interface

This section describes standards for the capitalization of text in the Java look and feel. Text is an important design element and appears throughout your application in such components as command buttons, checkboxes, radio buttons, alert box messages, and labels for groups of interface elements. Strive to be concise and consistent with language.

☕ For all text that appears in the interface elements of your application, follow one of two capitalization conventions: headline capitalization or sentence capitalization. Use headline capitalization for most names, titles, labels, and short text. Use sentence capitalization for lengthy text messages.

☕ Do not capitalize words automatically. You might encounter situations in your interface when capitalization is not appropriate, as in window titles for documents users have named without using capitalization.

🌐 Use standard typographical conventions for sentences and headlines in your application components. Let translators determine the standards in your target locales.

🌐 Place all text in resource bundles so that localization experts don't have to change your application's source code to accommodate translation.

Headline Capitalization in English

Most items in your application interface should use headline capitalization, which is the style traditionally used for book titles (and the section titles in this book). Capitalize every word except articles ("a," "an," and "the"), coordinating conjunctions (for example, "and," "or," "but," "so," "yet," and "nor"), and prepositions with fewer than four letters (like "in"). The first and last words are always capitalized, regardless of what they are.

Use headline capitalization for the following interface elements (examples are in parentheses):

- Checkbox text (Automatic Save Every Five Minutes)
- Combo box labels and text (Ruler Units:, Centimeters)
- Command button text (Don't Save)
- Icon names (Trash Can)
- Labels for groups of buttons or controls (New Contribution To:)
- Menu items (Save As...)
- Menu titles (View)

- Radio button text (Start at Top)
- Slider text (Left)
- Tab names (RGB Color)
- Text field labels (Appreciation Rate:)
- Titles of windows, panes, and dialog boxes (Color Chooser)
- Tool tips (Cut Selection)

If your tool tips are longer than a few words, sentence capitalization is acceptable. Be consistent within your application.

Sentence Capitalization in English   When text is in the form of full sentences, capitalize only the first word of each sentence (unless the text contains proper nouns, proper adjectives, or acronyms that are always capitalized). Avoid the use of long phrases that are not full sentences.

Use sentence capitalization in the following interface elements (examples are in parentheses):

- Dialog box text (The document you are closing has unsaved changes.)
- Error or help messages (The printer is out of paper.)
- Labels that indicate changes in status (Operation is 75% complete.)

Layout and Visual Alignment   Give careful consideration to the
layout of components in your windows and dialog boxes. A clear and consistent layout streamlines the way users move through an application and helps them utilize its features efficiently. The best designs are aesthetically pleasing and easy to understand. They orient components in the direction in which people read them, and they group together logically related components.

NOTE – Throughout this book, the spacing illustrations for all user interface elements use pixels as the unit of measurement. A screen at approximately 72 to 100 pixels per inch is assumed.

When you lay out your components, remember that users might use the mouse, keyboard, or an assistive technology to navigate through them; therefore, use a logical order (for instance, place the most important elements within a dialog box first in reading order).

Between-Component Padding and Spacing Guidelines   Use multiples of 6 pixels
for perceived spacing between components. If the measurement involves a
component edge with a white border, subtract 1 pixel to arrive at the actual
measurement between components (because the white border on active
components is less visually significant than the dark border). In these cases,
you should specify the actual measurement as 1 pixel less—that is, 5 pixels
between components within a group and 11 pixels between groups of
components.

NOTE – Exceptions to these spacing guidelines are noted in the relevant
component chapters in Part III. For instance, the perceived spacing between
toolbar buttons is 3 pixels, whereas the actual spacing is 2 pixels.

In the following figure, a perceived 6-pixel vertical space is actually 5 pixels
between checkbox components. The figure also shows how the perceived
spacing between inactive objects is preserved. Note that the dimensions of
inactive components are the same as active objects, although the white
border of active objects is replaced by an invisible 1-pixel border on the
bottom and right side of inactive objects.

FIGURE 27   Perceived and Actual Spacing of Active and Inactive Components

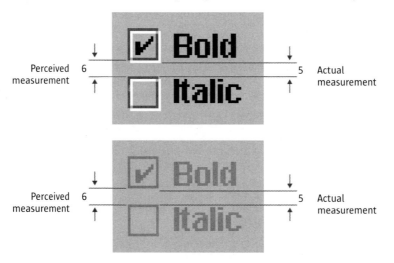

Insert 5 pixels (6 minus 1) between closely related items such as
grouped checkboxes. Insert 11 pixels (12 minus 1) for greater separation
between sets of components (such as between a group of radio buttons and a

group of checkboxes). Insert 12 pixels between items that don't have the flush 3D border highlight (for instance, text labels, titled borders, and padding at the top and left edges of a pane).

For guidelines on the spacing of individual JFC components with the Java look and feel, see "Toolbar Button Spacing and Padding" on page 143, "Command Button Spacing" on page 151, "Radio Button Spacing" on page 156, and "Checkbox Spacing" on page 154.

Design Grids   The most effective method of laying out user interface elements is to use a design grid with blank space to set apart logically related sets of components. A grid divides the available space into areas that can help you to arrange and align components in a pleasing layout. Grids make it easy for users to see the logical sequence of tasks and to understand the relationships between sets of components.

The following illustration shows a sample grid that provides standard margins and divides the remaining space into five columns. Horizontal divisions aid in scanning and interpreting the components and sets of related options.

⊕ Use the appropriate layout manager to control horizontal space for the variable width of internationalized text strings.

FIGURE 28   Grid With Horizontal Divisions

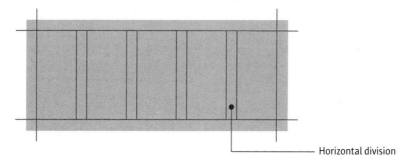

Horizontal division

You can use the number and width of components and their associated labels to determine the number of columns in a grid. At the beginning of the design process, vertical divisions are more difficult to set because they depend on the depth of components and sets of components, which are not yet placed.

Developing a grid is an ongoing process. If you know how much space is available, you can start working with the components to determine the most effective use of space. A grid can also help you to determine how much space to allocate to a given set of components. If you can define a grid that will work for a number of layouts, your application will have a more consistent appearance.

For spacing between rows and columns, use multiples of 6 pixels minus 1, to allow for the flush 3D border (see "Between-Component Padding and Spacing Guidelines" on page 48).

⊟⊸ Design grids are not to be confused with the AWT Grid Layout Manager.

Layout of a Simple Dialog Box   The following illustrations show steps in the process of using a grid to lay out a simple find dialog box.

First, determine the functional requirements. Then add the components according to the Java look and feel placement and spacing standards. For instance, you must right-align command buttons in dialog boxes at the bottom and separate them vertically from the rest of the components by 17 pixels.

FIGURE 29   Vertical Separation of Command Buttons

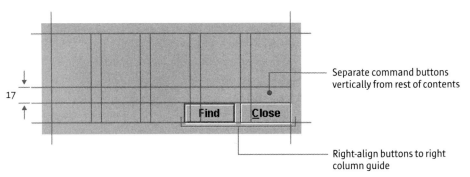

Separate command buttons vertically from rest of contents

Right-align buttons to right column guide

Using the grid as a guide, add the rest of the components. Place the most important options, or those you expect users to complete first, prior to others in reading order.

In the following illustration, the most important option—the text field for the search string—has been placed first. Related options are aligned with it along one of the column guides. Spacing between components and groups of components follows the Java look and feel standards.

FIGURE 30   Vertical Separation of Component Groups

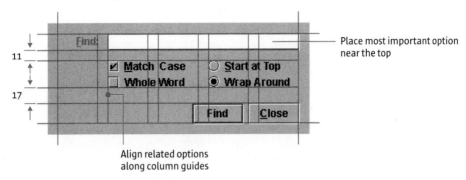

Titled Borders for Panels   The JFC enables you to specify a titled border for panels, which you can use as containers for components inside your application's windows.

FIGURE 31   Spacing for a Panel With Titled Border

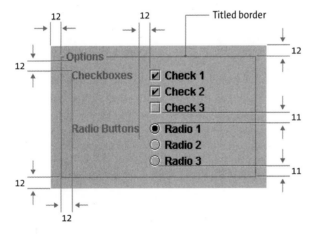

☕ Since titled borders take up considerable space, do not use them to supply titles for components; use labels instead.

☕ Use a titled border in a panel to group two or more sets of related components, but do not draw titled borders around a *single* set of checkboxes or radio buttons.

☕ Use titled borders sparingly: they are best when you must emphasize one group of components or separate one group of components from other components in the same window. Do not use multiple rows and columns of titled borders; they can be distracting and more confusing than simply grouping the elements with a design grid.

☕ Never nest titled borders. It becomes difficult to see the organizational structure of the panel and too many lines cause distracting optical effects.

☕ Insert 12 pixels between the edges of the panel and the titled border. Insert 12 pixels between the bottom of the title and the top of the first label (as well as between the label and the components) in the panel. Insert 11 pixels between component groups and between the bottom of the last component and the lower border.

🌐 Allow for internationalized titles and labels in panels that use titled borders.

▤▷ A titled border can be created as follows:

```
myPanel.setBorder(new TitledBorder(new LineBorder
(MetalLookAndFeel.getControlShadow()),
"<< Your Text Here >>"));
```

Text Layout   Text is an important design element in your layouts. The way you align and lay out text is vital to the appearance and ease of use of your application. The most significant layout issues with respect to text are label orientation and alignment.

☕ Use language that is clear, consistent, and concise throughout your application text. Moreover, ensure that the wording of your labels, component text, and instructions is legible and grammatically correct.

Label Orientation   You indicate a label's association with a component when you specify its relative position. Hence, consistency and clarity are essential. In the following figure, the label appears before and at the top of the list in reading order.

FIGURE 32   Label Orientation

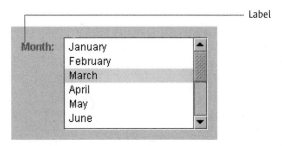

In general, orient labels before the component to which they refer, in reading order for the current locale. For instance, in the U.S. locale, place labels above or to the left of the component. Positioning to the left is preferable, since it allows for separation of text and components into discrete columns. This practice helps users read and understand the options.

Label Alignment   Between components, alignment of multiple labels becomes an issue. Aligning labels to a left margin can make them easier to scan and read. It also helps to give visual structure to a block of components, particularly if there is no immediate border (such as a window frame) surrounding them. If labels vary greatly in length, the use of right alignment can make it easier to determine the associated component; however, this practice also introduces large areas of negative space, which can be unattractive. The use of concise wording in labels can help to alleviate such difficulties. For an example of right-aligned labels in an applet, see Figure 12 on page 11.

Align labels with the top of associated components.

Avoid the use of titled borders as organizing elements. They add clutter reduce readability, and compound alignment problems by introducing the title as an additional text label. Instead, use design grids and careful alignment of labels to give visual structure to your layouts.

To accommodate differences in languages, decide on the behavior you want to occur during resize operations. Be specific about layout, spacing, and ordering. Use the layout managers to accommodate these differences.

Since the length and height of translated text varies, use layout managers properly to allow for differences in labels.

Animation

If used appropriately, animation has great potential to be a useful and attractive part of a user interface. You can use animation to let users know that the system is busy with a task or to draw attention to important events.

☕ Do not overuse animation since it distracts users and draws attention away from other elements of your application.

▥▭ Screen readers, which are used by people with visual impairments, do not recognize images that move. Use the `accessibleDescription` field to describe what is represented by the animation.

Progress and Delay Indication

Animation is especially useful when you want to communicate that the system is busy. Progress indication shows users the state of an operation; delay indication lets users know that an application or a part of an application is not available until an operation is done.

Properly used, animation can be of minimal disruption to the user. Feedback lets users know the application has received their input and is operating on it.

☕ When the application is processing a long operation and users can continue to work in other areas of the application, provide them with information regarding the state of the process.

☕ During a long operation, when users must wait until the operation is complete, change the shape of the pointer.

For example, an application's pointer might change to the wait pointer after the user selects a file and before the file opens. For information on the JFC-supplied pointer shapes available in the Java look and feel, see Table 7 on page 79.

☕ If you know the estimated length of an operation (for example, if the user is copying files) or the number of operations, use the Java look and feel progress bar. This bar fills from left to right as the operation progresses, as shown in the following figure.

FIGURE 33   Animation in a Progress Dialog Box

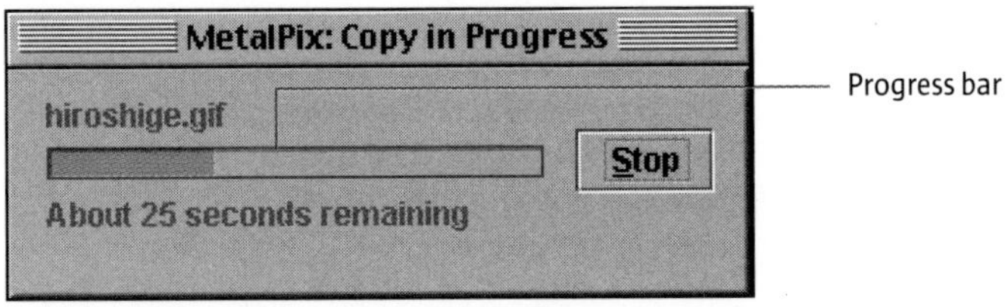

Progress bar

For more on progress bars, see "Progress Bars" on page 160.

Another way to indicate delay is to use animated pointers, which are supported by the Java 2 platform. Instead of just changing to a wait pointer, you can go one step further by animating the pointer image while the system is busy.

System Status Animation   Animation is useful when you want to call attention to events. For instance, in a mail application, you might use animation to indicate that new mail has arrived. Another example is a monitoring system that uses animation to alert users when failures occur.

When creating system status animation, consider the target users and their environment. If the animation needs to be visible from across the room, a bolder animation coupled with sound might be just the right thing. On the other hand, that same animation viewed by a user sitting at the workstation would be annoying.

When feasible, let users configure system status animation, so they can adapt their systems to the environment.

5: APPLICATION GRAPHICS

This chapter provides details on:

- The use of cross-platform color
- The design of application graphics, such as button graphics, icons, and symbols
- The use of graphics to enhance your product and corporate identity

Because the quality of your graphics can affect user confidence and even the perceived stability of your application, it is wise to seek the advice of a professional visual designer.

Working With Cross-Platform Color

In a cross-platform delivery environment, you need to ensure that the visual components of your application reproduce legibly and aesthetically on all your target systems. In many cases, you might not know which platforms will be used to run your software or what display capabilities they might have.

Online graphics consist of the visual representations of JFC components in the Java look and feel, which are drawn for you by the toolkit, and application graphics such as icons and splash screens, which you supply.

The Java look and feel components use a simple color model that reproduces well even on displays with a relatively small number of available colors. You can use the theme mechanism to change the colors of the components. For details, see "Themes" on page 39.

☕ Use themes to control the colors of Java look and feel components—for instance, to provide support for display devices with minimal available colors (fewer than 16 colors).

You need to supply icons, button graphics, pictures and logos for splash screens, and About boxes. Since these graphics might be displayed on a number of different platforms and configurations, you must develop a strategy for ensuring a high quality of reproduction.

☕ Use color only as a secondary means of representing important information. Make use of other characteristics (shape, texture, size, or intensity contrast) that do not require color vision or a color monitor.

The colors available on your users' systems, along with graphic file formats, determine how accurately the colors you choose are displayed on screen. Judging color availability is difficult, especially when you are designing applications to be delivered on multiple configurations or platforms.

Working With Available Colors   The number of colors available on a system is determined by the **bit depth**, which is the number of bits of information used to represent a single pixel on the monitor. The lowest number of bits used for modern desktop color monitors is usually 8 bits (256 colors); 16 bits provide for thousands of colors (65,536, to be exact); and 24 bits, common on newer systems, provide for millions of colors (16,777,216). The specific colors available on a system are determined by the way in which the target platform allocates colors. Available colors might differ from application to application.

Designers sometimes use predefined color palettes when producing images. For example, some web designers work within a set of 216 "web-safe" colors. These colors reproduce in many web browsers without **dithering** (as long as the system is capable of displaying at least 256 colors). Dithering occurs when a system or application attempts to simulate an unavailable color by using a pattern of two or more colors or shades from the system palette.

Outside web browsers, available colors are not so predictable. Individual platforms have different standard colors or deal with palettes in a dynamic way. The web-safe colors might dither when running in a standalone application, or even in an applet within a browser that usually does not dither these colors. Since the colors available to a Java application can differ each time it is run, especially across platforms, you cannot always avoid dithering in your images.

🖳🖥 Identify and understand the way that your target platforms handle colors at different bit depths. To achieve your desired effect, test your graphics on all target platforms at depths less than 16 bits.

Choosing Graphic File Formats   You can use two graphic file formats for images on the Java platform: **GIF** (Graphics Interchange Format) and **JPEG** (named after its developers, the Joint Photographic Experts Group).

GIF is the common format for application graphics in the Java look and feel. GIF files tend to be smaller on disk and in memory than JPEG files. Each GIF image is limited to 256 colors, or 8 bits of color information per pixel. A GIF file includes a list (or palette) of the colors (256 or fewer) used in the image. The number of colors in the palette and the complexity of the image are two factors that affect the size of the graphic file.

On 8-bit systems, some of the colors specified in a GIF file will be unavailable if they are not part of the system's current color palette. These unavailable colors will be dithered by the system. On 16-bit and 24-bit systems, more colors are available and different sets of colors can be used in different GIF files. Each GIF image, however, is still restricted to a set of 256 colors.

JPEG graphics are generally better suited for photographs than for the more symbolic style of icons, button graphics, and corporate type and logos. JPEG graphics use a compression algorithm that yields varying image quality depending on the compression setting, whereas GIF graphics use lossless compression that preserves the appearance of the original 8-bit image.

Choosing Colors   At monitor depths greater than 8 bits, most concerns about how any particular color reproduces become less significant. Any system capable of displaying thousands (16 bits) or millions (24 bits) of colors can find a color very close to, or exactly the same as, each value defined in a given image. Newer systems typically display a minimum of thousands of colors. Different monitors and different platforms might display the same color differently, however. For instance, a given color in one GIF file might look different to the eye from one system to another.

Many monitors or systems still display only 256 colors. For users with these systems, it might be advantageous to use colors known to exist in the system palette of the target platforms. Most platforms include a small set of "reserved" colors that are always available. Unfortunately, these reserved colors are often not useful for visual design purposes or for interface elements because they are highly saturated (the overpowering hues one might expect to find in a basic box of magic markers). Furthermore, there is little overlap between the reserved color sets of different platforms, so reserved colors are not guaranteed to reproduce without dithering across platforms.

Select colors that do not overwhelm the content of your application or distract users from their tasks. Stay away from saturated hues. For the sake of visual appeal and ease of use, choose groups of muted tones for your interface elements.

Since there is no lowest-common-denominator solution for choosing common colors across platforms (or even colors that are guaranteed to reproduce on a single platform), some of the colors in your application graphics will dither when running in 8-bit color. The best strategy is to design images that dither gracefully, as described in the following section.

Maximizing Color Quality   Images with fine color detail often reproduce better on 8-bit systems than those images that are mapped to a predefined palette (such as the web-safe palette) and use large areas of solid colors. Dithering in small areas is less noticeable than it is over larger areas, and, for isolated pixels of a given color, dithering simply becomes color substitution. Often colors in the system palette can provide a fair-to-good match with those specified in a GIF file. The overall effect of color substitution in small areas can be preferable to the dithering patterns produced for single colors, or to the limited number of colors resulting from pre-mapping to a given color palette.

The following table shows a graphic with a blur effect that contains a large number of grays. Remapping this graphic to the web-safe palette reduces the number of grays to two and results in an unpleasing approximation of the original graphic. However, the original GIF file displays acceptably in a Java application running in 8-bit color on various operating systems, even though the systems might not have available the exact colors in the image.

TABLE 4   Remappings of a Blurred Graphic

	Original Graphic	Microsoft Windows	Macintosh	CDE
Original colors				
Remapped to web-safe palette				

There are no absolutely safe cross-platform colors. Areas of solid color often dither, producing distracting patterns. One effective way to avoid coarse dithering patterns is to "pre-dither" your artwork intentionally. This approach minimizes obvious patterned dithering on 8-bit systems while still permitting very pleasing effects on systems capable of displaying more than 256 colors.

To achieve this effect, overlay a semitransparent checkerboard pattern on your graphics. The following figure shows how to build a graphic using this technique.

FIGURE 34 Adding a Pattern to Avoid Coarse Dithering Patterns

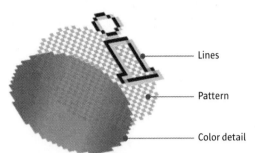

Lines

Pattern

Color detail

To build the graphic:

1. Use a graphics application with layers.

2. Apply the pattern only to areas that might dither badly. Leave borders and other detail lines as solid colors.

3. Play with the transparency setting for the pattern layer until the pattern is dark enough to mix with the color detail without overwhelming it visually. A 25% transparency with the default secondary 2 color (RGB 153-153-153) produces a good result for most graphics.

4. Test your results on your target 8-bit platforms.

The following table shows the variable results of graphic reproduction in 8-bit color, using different styles for various operating systems.

TABLE 5 Variations in Reproduction of 8-Bit Color

Styles	Original Graphic	Windows 95 (8 bits)	Mac OS 8.5 (8 bits)	CDE (8 bits)
Plain				
Dithering added				
Gradient				
Dithering added to gradient				

lain graphic in the preceding table, which uses a large area of a single eb-safe color, dithers badly on Windows 95 and CDE. Adding a pattern to the plain color improves the appearance only slightly. A gradient effect is added to the graphic to add some visual interest; this produces a banding effect on Mac OS 8.5. Adding the dithered pattern produces good results on all three platforms with 8-bit color. In 16-bit and 24-bit color, the graphic reproduction is very close to, or exactly the same as, the originals.

Designing Graphics in the Java Look and Feel Style

Application graphics that you design fall into three broad categories:

- Icons, which represent objects that users can select, open, or drag
- Button graphics, which identify actions, settings, and tools (modes of the application)
- Symbols, which are used for general identification and labeling (for instance, as indicators of conditions or states)

TABLE 6 Examples of Application Graphics

Graphic Type	Examples	Basic 3D Style	Pre-Dithered
Icons	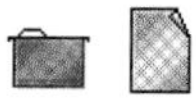		
Button graphics	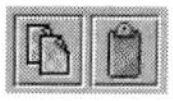		
Symbols			

Use the GIF file format for iconic and symbolic graphics. It usually results in a smaller file size than the JPEG format and uses lossless compression.

Put all application graphics in resource bundles.

Where possible, use globally understood icons, button graphics, and symbols. Where none exist, create them with input from international sources. If you can't create a single symbol that works in all cultures, define appropriate graphics for different locales (but try to minimize this task).

Designing Icons

Icons typically represent containers, documents, network objects, or other data that users can open or manipulate within an application. An **icon** usually appears with identifying text.

The two standard sizes for icons are 16 x 16 pixels and 32 x 32 pixels. The smaller size is more common and is used in JFC components such as the internal frame (to identify the contents of the window or minimized internal frame) and tree view (for container and leaf nodes). You can use 32 x 32 icons for applications designed for users with visual impairments or for objects in a diagram, such as a network topology.

☕ Design icons to identify clearly the objects or concepts they represent. Keep the drawing style symbolic, as opposed to photo-realistic. Too much detail can make it more difficult for users to recognize what the icon represents.

☕ When designing large and small icons that represent the same object, make sure that they have similar shape, color, and detail.

☕ Specify values for the `accessibleDescription` and `accessibleName` properties for each icon so that assistive technologies can find out what it is and how to use it.

Working With Icon Styles

The following figure shows sample 32 x 32 and 16 x 16 icons for files and folders drawn in two different styles. Note that many objects are difficult to draw in a flush 3D style, particularly at the smaller 16 x 16 size. Three visual elements appear in the sample icons: an interior highlight (to preserve the flush style used throughout the Java look and feel), a pattern to minimize dithering (described in "Working With Available Colors" on page 58), and a dark border.

FIGURE 35   Two Families of Icons

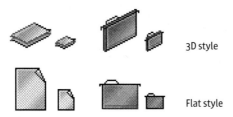

3D style

Flat style

☕ Use a single style to create a "family" of icons that utilize common visual elements to reflect similar concepts, roles, and identity. Icons in families might use a similar palette, size, and style.

☕ Don't mix two- and three-dimensional styles in the same icon family.

☕ For satisfactory display on a wide range of background colors and textures, use a clear, dark exterior border and ensure that there is no anti-aliasing or other detail around the perimeter of the graphic.

Drawing Icons   The following section uses a simple folder as an example of how to draw an icon. Before you start, decide on a general design for the object. In this example, a hanging file folder is used to represent a directory.

1. Draw a basic outline shape first.

   Icons can use as much of the available space as possible, since they are displayed without borders. Icons should usually be centered horizontally in the available space. For vertical spacing, consider aligning to the baseline of other icons in the set, or aligning with text (for instance, in a tree).

   If both sizes are required, work on them at the same time rather than trying to scale down a detailed 32 x 32 icon later; both sizes then can evolve into designs that are recognizable as the same object.

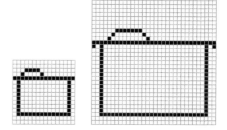

2. Add some basic color (green is used here).

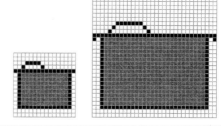

3. Draw a highlight on the inside top and left.

   This practice creates the flush 3D style of the Java look and feel.

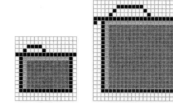

4. Add some detail to the icon.

   In this case, the crease or "fold" mark in the hanging folder is drawn.

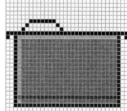

5. Try a gradient that produces a "shining" effect instead of the flat green.

   Here a dark green has replaced the black border on the right and bottom; black is not a requirement as long as there is a well-defined border.

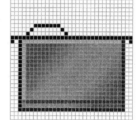

6. Add a pattern to prevent coarse dithering. This technique minimizes banding and dithering on displays with 256 or fewer colors (see "Maximizing Color Quality" on page 60).

   The first graphic is an exploded view of an icon that shows how the pattern is added.

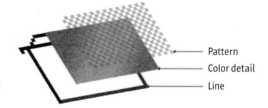

Pattern

Color detail

Line

The next graphic shows an icon in which a pattern has been added to the color detail.

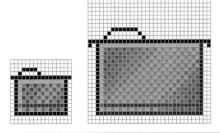

7. Define the empty area around the icon graphic (in which you have not drawn anything) as transparent pixels in the GIF file.

   This practice ensures that the background color shows through; if the icon is dragged to or displayed on a different background, the area surrounding it matches the color or pattern of the rest of the background.

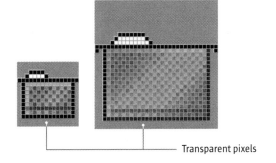

Transparent pixels

Designing Button Graphics

Button graphics appear inside buttons—most often in toolbar buttons. Such graphics identify the action, setting, mode, or other function represented by the button. For instance, clicking the button might carry out an action (creating a new file) or set a state (boldfaced text).

The two standard sizes for button graphics are 16 x 16 pixels and 24 x 24 pixels. Either size (but not both at the same time) can be used in toolbars or tool palettes, depending on the amount of space available. For details on toolbars, see "Toolbars" on page 140. For more on palette windows, see "Palettes" on page 110.

If you include both text and graphics in a button, the size of the button will exceed 16 x 16 or 24 x 24 pixels. If the button size is an issue, consider using tool tips instead.

⊕ Do not include text as part of your button graphics (GIF files). Use button text instead. Keep the button text in a resource bundle to facilitate localization.

Note, however, that toolbar buttons can display text instead of graphics, particularly if your usability testing establishes that the action, state, or mode represented by the button graphic is difficult for users to comprehend. Tool tips for toolbar buttons can help clarify the meaning of a button. For details, see "Tool Tips for Toolbar Buttons" on page 144.

☕ When designing your button graphics, clearly show the action, state, or mode that the button initiates.

☕ Keep the drawing style symbolic; too much detail can make it more difficult for users to understand what a button does.

☕ Use a flush 3D border to indicate that a button is clickable.

☕ Draw a clear, dark border without anti-aliasing or other exterior detail (except the flush 3D highlight) around the outside of a button graphic.

Using Button Graphic Styles

The following figure shows sample button graphics designed for toolbars and for the contents of a tool palette.

FIGURE 36 Button Graphics for a Toolbar and a Tool Palette

☕ Use a single style to create a "family" of button graphics with common visual elements. You might use a similar palette, size, and style for different button groups, such as toolbar buttons, toggle buttons, or command buttons. Review the graphics in context before finalizing them.

Producing the Flush 3D Effect

To produce the flush 3D effect, add an exterior white highlight on the outside right and bottom of the graphic and an interior highlight on the inside left and top.

FIGURE 37 Flush 3D Effect in a Button Graphic

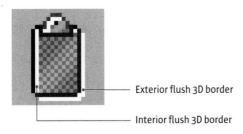

———— Exterior flush 3D border

———— Interior flush 3D border

Working With Button Borders   The size of a button graphic includes all the pixels within the border. As shown in the following illustration, horizontal and vertical dimensions are both either 24 or 16 pixels. The border abuts the button graphic (that is, there are no pixels between the border and the graphic).

FIGURE 38   Button Graphics With Borders

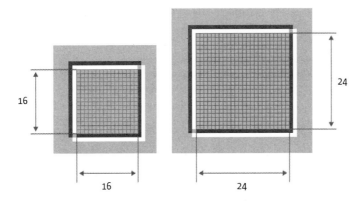

Determining the Primary Drawing Area   Because the white pixels in both the button border and the button graphic are less visually significant than the darker borders, the area used for most of the drawing is offset within the 16 x 16 or 24 x 24 space. The following illustration shows the standard drawing area for both button sizes. Note that the white highlight used to produce the flush 3D style in the button graphic might fall outside this area.

FIGURE 39   Primary Drawing Area in Buttons

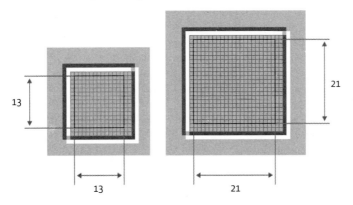

The following illustrations show 16 x 16 and 24 x 24 button graphics that use the maximum recommended drawing area. Notice that on all sides there are 2 pixels between the dark border of the button graphic and the dark portion of the button border.

FIGURE 40   Maximum-Size Button Graphics

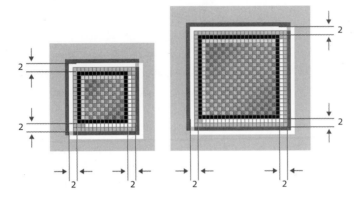

Drawing the Button Graphic   When drawing a button graphic, first decide on a general design that represents the action or setting activated by the button. In the following examples, a clipboard suggests the Paste command.

1. Decide which size you want to use for the button or toolbar graphic.

2. Draw a basic outline shape, taking care to remain within the primary drawing area.

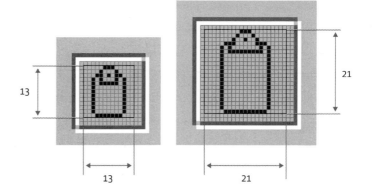

3. Add some basic color.

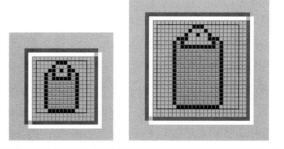

4. Add the flush 3D effect by drawing highlights on the inside left and top, and on the outside bottom and right of the outline.

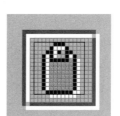

This is a good basic design, but because of the large area using a single color, the graphic lacks visual interest and might not reproduce well on some systems.

5. Try a gradient instead
   of the flat color.

6. Add a pattern. This
   technique minimizes
   banding and
   dithering on displays
   with 256 or fewer
   colors (see
   "Maximizing Color
   Quality" on page 60).

Pattern

Color detail

Lines

The first figure shows
an exploded view of
the button graphic
without flush 3D
highlights. The next
figure shows the
effect of the pattern
on the color detail of
the button graphic.

7. Define the empty area around your button graphic (in which you have not drawn anything) as transparent pixels in the GIF file.

This practice ensures that the background color shows through; if the theme changes, the area around the button graphic will match the rest of the background canvas in the interface.

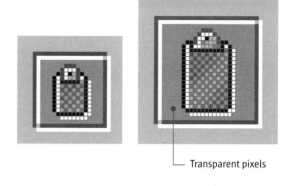

Transparent pixels

Designing Symbols

Symbols include any small graphic (typically 48 x 48 pixels or smaller) that stands for a state or a concept but has no directly associated action or object. Symbols might appear within dialog boxes, system status alert boxes, and event logs. Saturated colors might be useful for status or warning symbols.

The examples in the following figure show the graphic from an Info alert box and a caution symbol superimposed on a folder icon to indicate a hypothetical state. The style for symbols is not as narrowly defined as that for icons and button graphics. The examples in the following figure use a flush or etched effect for interior detail but not for the border of the graphic.

FIGURE 41   Symbols

Information symbol   Caution symbol

☕ Ensure adequate contrast between a warning symbol and the icon or background it appears against.

Designing Graphics for Corporate and Product Identity

Application graphics present an excellent opportunity for you to enhance your corporate or product identity. This section presents information about installation screens, splash screens, About boxes, and login splash screens.

NOTE – The examples presented in this section use the sample text-editing and mail applications, MetalEdit and MetalMail. They are not appropriate for third-party use.

☕ Use the JPEG file format for any photographic elements in your installation screens, splash screens, and About boxes.

Designing Installation Screens An installation screen is a window containing images that are displayed in an application installer. Often the first glimpse users have of your application is the installer. Consequently, an installation screen introduces and reinforces your corporate and product identity. The number of screens in an installer can vary.

☕ Use a plain window for installation screens, and draw any desired border inside the window.

☕ Provide a clearcut way for your users to move through the steps required to perform the installation, and enable them to cancel or stop the installation at any point.

⊞▭ The JWindow component is typically used to implement plain windows.

See "Layout and Visual Alignment" on page 47 for general guidelines on how to arrange and align items.

Designing Splash Screens A splash screen is a plain window that appears briefly in the time between the launch of a program and the appearance of its main application window. Nothing other than a blank space is included with a JFC-supplied plain window; you must provide the border and the contents of the splash screen. For instance, the black border on the window in the following figure is part of the GIF file supplied by the splash screen designer.

FIGURE 42   Splash Screen for MetalEdit

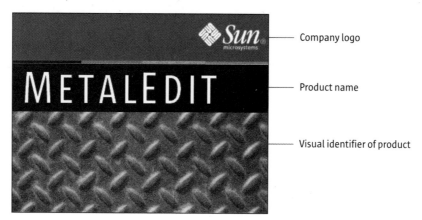

Although not required, splash screens are included in most commercial products. Splash screens typically have the following elements:

- Company logo
- Product name (trademarked, if appropriate)
- Visual identifier of the product or product logo

Check with your legal adviser about requirements for placing copyright notices or other legal information in your splash screens.

To get the black border that is recommended for splash screens, you must include a 1-pixel black border as part of the image you create.

The JWindow component, not the JFrame component, is typically used to implement the plain window that provides the basis for splash screens.

Designing Login Splash Screens If your application requires users to log in, you might consider replacing the traditional splash screen with a login splash screen.

FIGURE 43 Login Splash Screen for MetalMail

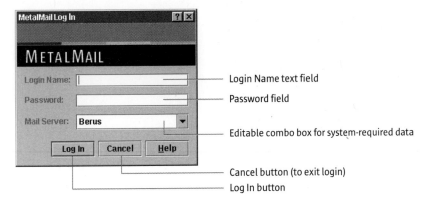

The elements of this screen might include:

- Label and text field for a login user name
- Label and password field
- Label and editable combo box for any other information required by the system
- Buttons for logging in and canceling the login splash screen

To save time and to increase the chance of users viewing a splash screen, it is a good idea to combine your login screen and your splash screen.

Provide a way for users to exit the login splash screen without first logging in.

The JDialog component, not the JWindow component, is typically used to implement a login splash screen.

Designing About Boxes   An About box is a dialog box that contains basic
information about your application.

FIGURE 44   About Box for MetalEdit

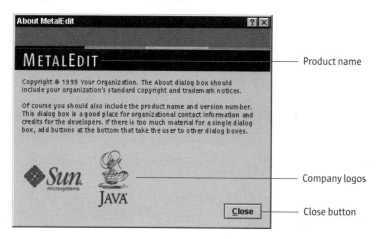

An About box might contain the following elements:

- Product name (trademarked, if appropriate)
- Version number
- Company logo
- Product logo or a visual reminder of the product logo
- Copyright, trademarks, and other legal notices
- Names of contributors to the product

Because users typically display About boxes by choosing the About
Application item from the Help menu, be sure that the About box is
accessible while your application is running.

Because the dialog box title bar may not include a Close button on all
platforms, include a Close button in your About boxes so that users can
dismiss them after reading them. Follow the guidelines for button placement
described in "Spacing in Dialog Boxes" on page 115.

6: BEHAVIOR

Users interact with the computer via the mouse, the keyboard, and the screen. Such interaction is the "feel" portion of the Java look and feel. This chapter provides input guidelines and recommendations for interaction techniques. It describes mouse operations, including information on pointers, and drag-and-drop operations. It also discusses keyboard operations, including the use of mnemonics, keyboard shortcuts, and keyboard focus in Java look and feel applications.

Mouse Operations
In Java look and feel applications, the following common mouse operations are available to users:

- Moving the mouse changes the position of the onscreen **pointer** (often called the "cursor").

- Clicking (pressing and releasing a mouse button) selects or activates the object beneath the pointer. The object is usually highlighted when the mouse button is pressed and then selected or activated when the mouse button is released. For example, a click is used to activate a command button, to select an item from a list, or to set an insertion point in a text area.

- Double-clicking (clicking a mouse button twice in rapid succession without moving the mouse) is used to select larger units (for example, to select a word in a text field) or to select and open an object.

- Triple-clicking (clicking a mouse button three times in rapid succession without moving the mouse) is used to select even larger units (for instance, to select an entire line in a text field).

- Dragging (pressing a mouse button, moving the mouse, and releasing the mouse button) is used to select a range of objects, to choose items from drop-down menus, or to move objects in the interface.

In your design, assume a two-button mouse. Use **mouse button 1** (usually the left button) for selection, activation of components, dragging, and the display of drop-down menus. Use **mouse button 2** (usually the right button) to display contextual menus. Do not use the **middle mouse button**; it is not available on most target platforms.

⊟⊡ Be aware that Macintosh systems usually have a one-button mouse, other personal computers and network computers usually have a two-button mouse, and UNIX systems usually have a three-button mouse.

☕ Restrict interaction to the use of mouse button 1 and mouse button 2. Macintosh users can simulate mouse button 2 by holding down the Control key while using mouse button 1.

The following figure shows the relative placement of mouse buttons 1 and 2 on Macintosh, PC, and UNIX mouse devices.

FIGURE 45   Cross-Platform Mouse Buttons and Their Default Assignments

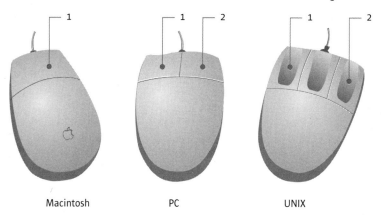

Macintosh   PC   UNIX

Pointer Feedback   The pointer can assume a variety of shapes. For instance, in a text-editing application, the pointer might assume an I-beam shape (called a "text pointer" in the JDK) to indicate where the insertion point will be if the user presses the mouse button. The **insertion point** is the location where typed text or a dragged or pasted selection will appear. When the pointer moves out of the editor pane, it returns to its initial appearance as a default pointer.

The Java look and feel defines a set of pointer types that map to the corresponding native platform pointers; therefore, the appearance of pointers can vary from platform to platform, as shown in the following table. When no corresponding pointer exists in the native platform toolkit, the pointer is supplied by the JFC.

TABLE 7   Pointer Types Available in JDK 1.1 and the Java 2 SDK

Pointer	Macintosh	Windows 95	CDE	Usage in Java Look and Feel Applications
Default				Pointing, selecting, or moving
Crosshair	+	+	+	Interacting with graphic objects
Hand				Panning objects by direct manipulation
Move				Moving objects
Text	I	I	I	Selecting or inserting text
Wait				Indicating that an operation is in progress and the user cannot do other tasks
S Resize				Adjusting the lower (southern) border of an object
N Resize				Adjusting the upper (northern) border of an object
E Resize				Adjusting the right (eastern) border of an object
W Resize				Adjusting the left (western) border of an object
NW Resize				Adjusting the upper-left (northwest) corner of an object
NE Resize				Adjusting the upper-right (northeast) corner of an object
SE Resize				Adjusting the lower-right (southeast) corner of an object
SW Resize				Adjusting the lower-left (southwest) corner of an object

In addition to the shapes in Table 7, a pointer graphic can be defined as an image and created using `Toolkit.createCustomCursor` if you are using the Java 2 platform.

Mouse-over Feedback   Mouse-over feedback is a visual effect that occurs when users move the pointer over an area of an application window.

In the Java look and feel, **mouse-over feedback** can be used to show borders on toolbar buttons when the pointer moves over them. A slightly different effect is used to display tool tips. For details, see "Toolbars" on page 140 and "Tool Tips" on page 145.

Clicking and Selecting Objects   In the Java look and feel, the selection of objects with the mouse is similar to the standard practice for other graphical user interfaces. Users select an object by clicking it. Clicking an unselected object also deselects any previous selection.

JFC-provided text selection follows these general rules:

- A single click deselects any existing selection and sets the insertion point.

- A double click on a word deselects any existing selection and selects the word.

- A triple click in a line of text deselects any existing selection and selects the line.

- Dragging (that is, moving the mouse while holding down mouse button 1) through a range of text deselects any existing selection and selects the range.

JFC-provided selection in lists and tables follows these general rules:

- A click on an object deselects any existing selection and selects the object.

- A Shift-click on an object extends the selection from the most recently selected object to the current object.

- A Control-click on an object toggles its selection without affecting the selection of any other objects.

Displaying Contextual Menus   It can be difficult for users to find and access desired features given all the commands in the menus and submenus of a complex application. Contextual menus (sometimes called "pop-up menus") enable you to make such functions available throughout the graphical interface and to associate menu items with relevant objects.

Users can access contextual menus in two ways:

- To pull down the menu, users can press and hold mouse button 2 over a relevant object. Then they can drag to the desired menu item and release the mouse button to choose the item.

- To post the menu, users can click mouse button 2 over a relevant object. Then they can click the desired menu item to choose it.

FIGURE 46   Contextual Menu for a Text Selection

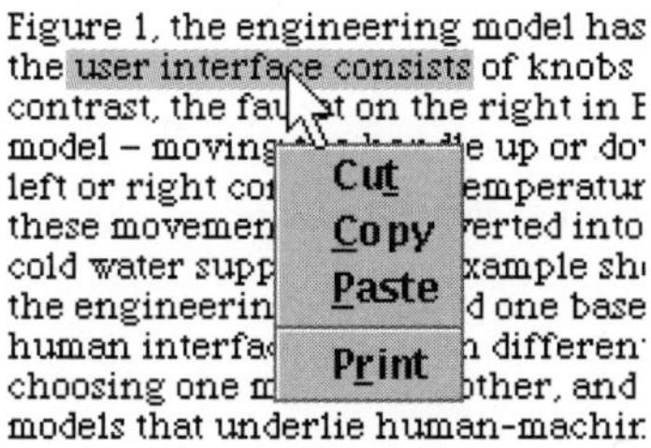

Figure 1, the engineering model has
the user interface consists of knobs
contrast, the fau st on the right in F
model – moving he up or do'
left or right co **Cut** emperatur
these movemen **Copy** verted into
cold water supp xample sh
the engineerin **Paste** d one base
human interfa h differen
choosing one m **Print** ther, and
models that underlie human-machir

Since users often have difficulty knowing whether contextual menus are available and what is in them, ensure that the items in your contextual menu also appear in the menu bar or toolbar of the primary windows in your application.

Be sure that the commands in your contextual menu apply only to a selected object or group of objects. For instance, a contextual menu might include cut, copy, and paste commands limited to a selected text range, as shown in the preceding figure.

Remember that users on the Microsoft Windows and UNIX platforms display a contextual menu by clicking or pressing mouse button 2. Macintosh users hold down the Control key while clicking.

Drag-and-Drop Operations

Drag-and-drop operations include moving, copying, or linking selected objects by dragging them from one location and dropping them over another. These operations provide a convenient and intuitive way to perform many tasks using direct manipulation. Common examples of **drag and drop** in the user interface are moving files by dragging file icons between folders or dragging selected text from one document to another. The Java 2 platform supports drag and drop between two Java applications or between a Java application and a native application. For example, on a Microsoft Windows system, users can drag a text selection from a Java application and drop it into a Microsoft Word document.

Typical Drag and Drop

Drag and drop in Java applications is similar to standard behavior on other platforms. Users press mouse button 1 while the pointer is over a source object and then drag the object by moving the pointer while holding down the mouse button. To drop the object, users release the button when the pointer is over a suitable destination. A successful drop triggers an action that depends on the nature of the source and destination. If the drag source is part of a range selection, the entire selection (for example, several file icons or a range of text) is dragged.

Pointer and Destination Feedback   During any drag-and-drop operation, your Java look and feel application needs to give visual feedback using the pointer and the destination.

☕ Provide the user with feedback that a drag operation is in progress by changing the shape of the pointer when the drag is initiated.

☕ Provide destination feedback so users know where the dragged object can be dropped. Use one or both of the following methods to provide destination feedback:

- Change the pointer shape to reflect whether the object is over a possible drop target.

- Highlight drop targets when the pointer is over them to indicate that they can accept the target.

▤▭ Java objects are specified by their **MIME** (Multipurpose Internet Mail Extensions) types, and the Java™ runtime environment automatically translates back and forth between MIME types and system-native types as needed. As an object is dragged over potential targets, each potential target can query the drag source to obtain a list of available data types and then compare that with the list of data types that it can accept. For example, when dragging a range of text, the source might be able to deliver the text in a number of different encodings or as plain text, styled text, or HTML text. If there is a match in data types, potential targets should be highlighted as the pointer passes over them to indicate that they can accept the dragged object.

Keyboard Operations   The Java look and feel assumes a PC-style keyboard. The standard ASCII keys are used, along with the following modifier keys: Shift, Control, and Alt (Option on the Macintosh); the function keys F1 through F12; the four arrow keys; Delete, Backspace, Home, End, Page Up, and Page Down. Enter and Return are equivalent. (Return does not appear on PC keyboards.)

A **modifier key** is a key that does not produce an alphanumeric character but can be used in combination with other keys to alter an action. Typical modifier keys in Java look and feel applications are Shift, Control, and Alt.

This section describes and provides recommendations for the use of **keyboard operations**, which include keyboard shortcuts, mnemonics, and other forms of navigation, selection, and activation that utilize the keyboard instead of the mouse. A **mnemonic** is an underlined letter that typically appears in a menu title, menu item, or the text of a button or other component. The underlined letter reminds users how to activate the equivalent command by pressing the Alt key and the character key that corresponds to the underlined letter. For instance, you could use a mnemonic to give keyboard focus to a text area or to activate a command button. A **keyboard shortcut** is a sequence of keys (such as Control-A) that activates a menu command.

Keyboard Focus

The **keyboard focus** (sometimes called "input focus") designates the active window or component where the user's next keystrokes will take effect. Focus typically moves when users click a component with a pointing device, but users can also control focus from the keyboard. Either way, users designate the window, or component within a window, that receives input. (There are exceptions: for instance, a left-alignment button on a toolbar should not take focus away from the text area where the actual work is taking place.)

When a window is first opened, assign initial keyboard focus to the component that would normally be used first. Often, this is the component appearing in the upper-left portion of the window. If keyboard focus is not assigned to a component in the active window, the keyboard navigation and control mechanisms cannot be used. The assignment of initial keyboard focus is especially important for people who use only a keyboard to navigate through your application—for instance, those with visual or mobility impairments.

In the Java look and feel, many components (including command buttons, checkboxes, radio buttons, toggle buttons, lists, combo boxes, tabbed panes, editable cells, and tree views) indicate keyboard focus by displaying a rectangular border (blue, in the default color theme).

FIGURE 47   Keyboard Focus Indicated by Rectangular Border

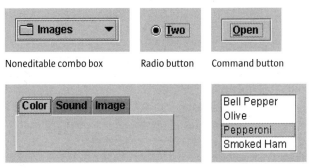

Noneditable combo box   Radio button   Command button

Tabbed pane   List

Table   Tree view

Editable text components, such as text fields, indicate keyboard focus by displaying a blinking bar at the insertion point.

FIGURE 48   Keyboard Focus Indicated by Blinking Bar at Insertion Point

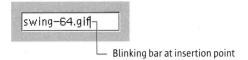

└─ Blinking bar at insertion point

Menus indicate focus with a colored background for menu titles or menu items (blue, in the default color theme).

FIGURE 49   Keyboard Focus Indicated by Colored Background

Drop-down menu

Split panes and sliders indicate focus by darkening the drag-textured areas (blue, in the default color theme).

FIGURE 50   Keyboard Focus Indicated by Drag Texture

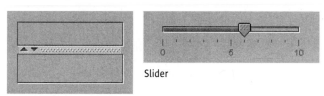

Slider

Split pane

Keyboard Navigation and Activation

Keyboard navigation and activation enable users to move keyboard focus from one user interface component to another via the keyboard.

In general, pressing the Tab key moves focus through the major components; Shift-Tab moves through the components in the reverse direction. Control-Tab and Control-Shift-Tab work in a similar fashion and are particularly useful when keyboard focus is in an element that accepts tabs, such as a text area or a table. Arrow keys are often used to move within groups of components — for example, Tab puts focus in a set of radio buttons and then the arrow keys move focus among the radio buttons. However, the Tab key is used to move among checkboxes.

Once an element has focus, pressing the spacebar typically activates it or selects it. In a list, pressing Shift-spacebar extends the selection; pressing Control-spacebar makes another selection without affecting the current selections.

Some components do not need explicit keyboard focus to be operated. For example, the default button in a dialog box can be operated by pressing the Enter or Return key without the default button having keyboard focus. Similarly, scrollbars can be operated from the keyboard if focus is anywhere within the scroll pane.

Keyboard navigation can be useful not only for accessibility purposes, but also for power users, users who prefer the keyboard over the mouse, or users who choose alternative input methods like voice input or onscreen keyboards.

☕ Ensure that all application functions are accessible from the keyboard by unplugging the mouse and testing the application's keyboard operations.

⊞⇨ Some of the keyboard operations in the tables in Appendix A are temporarily incomplete or unimplemented. However, the key sequences listed in this appendix should be reserved for future versions of the JFC and the Java 2 platform.

⊞⇨ The `setNextFocusableComponent` method from `JComponent` can be used to set the order for tabbing by chaining components together— specifying for each component what the next component in the sequence is.

The common operations for keyboard navigation and activation in the Java look and feel are summarized in the following table. Within the table, the term "group" refers to a group of toolbar buttons, menu titles, text, or table cells.

TABLE 8   Common Navigation and Activation Keys

Action	Keyboard Operation
Navigates in, navigates out	Tab[1]
Navigates out of a component that accepts tabs	Control-Tab[1]
Moves focus left one character or component within a group	Left arrow
Moves focus right one character or component within a group	Right arrow
Moves focus up one line or component within a group	Up arrow
Moves focus down one line or component within a group	Down arrow
Moves up one view	Page Up
Moves down one view	Page Down

TABLE 8   Common Navigation and Activation Keys *(Continued)*

Action	Keyboard Operation
Moves to the beginning of data; in a table, moves to the beginning of a line	Home
Moves to the end of data; in a table, moves to the last cell in a row	End
Activates the default command button	Enter or Return
Dismisses a menu or dialog box without changes	Escape
Activates or selects the component (with keyboard focus)	Spacebar

1. With Shift key, reverses direction

Keyboard Shortcuts   Keyboard shortcuts are keystroke combinations (consisting of a modifier key and a character key, like Control-Z) that activate a menu item from the keyboard even if the menu for that command is not currently displayed. Unlike mnemonics, keyboard shortcuts do not post menus; rather, they perform the indicated actions directly.

FIGURE 51   Edit Menu With Keyboard Shortcuts and Mnemonics

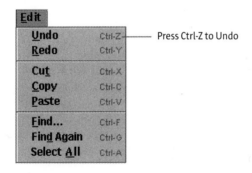

To use a keyboard shortcut in Java look and feel applications, users hold down the Control key (and optionally, an additional modifier key, such as Shift) and press the character key that is shown after the menu item. Typing the keyboard shortcut has the same effect as choosing the menu item. For instance, to undo an action, users can either choose the Undo item from the Edit menu or hold down the Control key and press Z.

Do not use the Meta key (the Command key on the Macintosh platform) for a keyboard shortcut, except as an alternate for Control. It is not available on many target platforms.

☕ Specify keyboard shortcuts for frequently used menu items to provide an alternative to mouse operation. The Java look and feel displays keyboard shortcuts using standard abbreviations for key names, separated by hyphens.

☕ Be aware of and use the common shortcuts across platforms that are summarized in the following table.

TABLE 9   Common Keyboard Shortcuts

Sequence	Equivalent
Ctrl-N	New (File menu)
Ctrl-O	Open (File menu)
Ctrl-S	Save (File menu)
Ctrl-P	Print (File menu)
Ctrl-W	Close (File menu)
Ctrl-Z	Undo (Edit menu)
Ctrl-Y	Redo (Edit menu)
Ctrl-X	Cut (Edit menu)
Ctrl-C	Copy (Edit menu)
Ctrl-V	Paste (Edit menu)
Ctrl-F	Find (Edit menu)
Ctrl-G	Find Again (Edit menu)
Ctrl-A	Select All (Edit menu)

🖵 Since keyboard shortcuts are not always equivalent on different platforms, ensure that any new keyboard shortcuts you have created are compatible with existing shortcuts on all your target platforms.

Mnemonics   Mnemonics provide yet another keyboard alternative to the mouse. A mnemonic is an underlined letter in a menu title, menu item, or other interface component. It reminds the user how to activate the equivalent command by simultaneously pressing the Alt key and the character key that corresponds to the underlined letter.

FIGURE 52   File Menu With Mnemonics and Keyboard Shortcuts

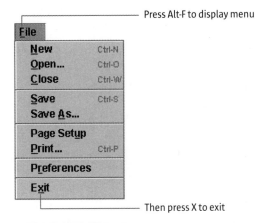

When keyboard focus is not in a text element, the Alt modifier is not always required. Menus are an example. For instance, to choose the Exit command from the File menu, the user can hold down the Alt key and press F to post the File menu, and then press X.

Once users have displayed a menu with a keyboard sequence, the subsequent key they press will activate a command only from that menu. Hence, users can press Alt-F to display the File menu and then type A to activate the Save As command, or press Alt-E to display the Edit menu, and then type A to activate the Select All command.

You can also provide mnemonics for components within the dialog boxes in your applications. However, it is important to note that this situation requires that you use a modifier key. For instance, within a dialog box, you might want to provide a mnemonic for the Help button. Once keyboard focus has moved within the dialog box, users press Alt, and then H to activate the Help button.

☕ Do not associate mnemonics with the default button or the Cancel button in a dialog box. Use Enter or Return for the default button and Escape for the Cancel button instead.

☕ Choose mnemonics that avoid conflicts. For instance, you cannot use the letter P as the mnemonic for both the Print and Page Setup commands.

☕ When you assign mnemonics, follow these guidelines in the specified order.

1. Use common mnemonics as they appear in Table 10 below.

2. If the mnemonic does not appear in the table of common mnemonics (Table 10), choose the first letter of the menu item. (For instance, choose J for Justify.)

3. If the first letter of the menu item conflicts with those of other items, choose a prominent consonant. (For instance, the letter S may have already been designated as the mnemonic for the Style command. Therefore, choose the letter Z as the mnemonic for the Size command.)

4. If the first letter of the menu item and the prominent consonant conflict with those of other menu items, choose a prominent vowel.

TABLE 10   Common Mnemonics

Menu Titles	Menu Items
File	New, Open, Close, Save, Save As, Page Setup, Print, Preferences, Exit
Edit	Undo, Redo, Cut, Copy, Paste, Find, Find Again, Select All
Help	Contents, Tutorial, Index, Search, About Application

▤▷ The `setMnemonic` method can be used to specify mnemonics on buttons, checkboxes, radio buttons, toggle buttons, and menu titles. The `setDisplayedMnemonic` method can be used for labels, and the `setAccelerator` method for menu items.

PART III: THE COMPONENTS OF THE JAVA FOUNDATION CLASSES

7: WINDOWS, PANES, AND FRAMES

Primary windows, secondary windows, utility windows, and plain windows provide the top-level containers for your application. A **primary window** is a window in which users' main interaction with the data or document takes place. An application can use any number of primary windows, which can be opened, closed, minimized, or resized independently. A **secondary window** is a supportive window that is dependent on a primary window (or another secondary window). In the secondary window, users can view and provide additional information about actions or objects in a primary window. A **utility window** is a window whose contents affect an active primary window. Unlike secondary windows, utility windows remain open when primary windows are closed or minimized. An example of a utility window is a tool palette that is used to select a graphic tool. A **plain window** is a window with no title bar or window controls, typically used for splash screens.

FIGURE 53   Primary, Utility, Plain, and Secondary Windows

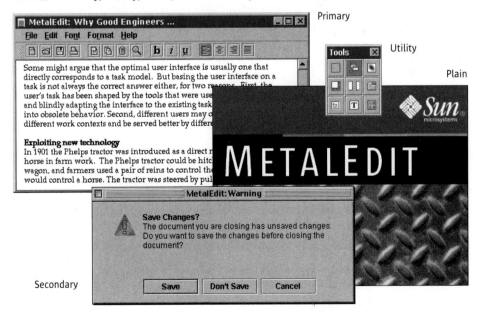

Similarly, as a designer you can use panels, panes, and internal frames as lower-level containers within primary and secondary windows. A **panel** is a container for organizing the contents of a window, dialog box, or applet. (You can place panels in panes or panes in panels.) A **pane** is a collective term for scroll panes, split panes, and tabbed panes, which are described in this chapter. An **internal frame** is a container used in MDI applications to create windows that users cannot drag outside of the desktop pane.

FIGURE 54   Scroll Pane, Tabbed Pane, Split Pane, and Internal Frame

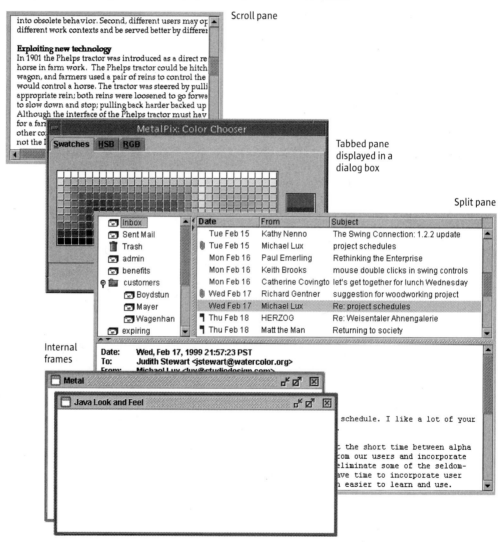

Anatomy of a Primary Window

Primary windows act as top-level containers for the user interface elements that appear inside them. A primary window might hold a series of embedded containers. For example, a primary window in your application could have this organization, as shown in the following figure:

- The window frame contains a menu bar and a panel
- The menu bar contains menus
- The panel contains a toolbar and a scroll pane and scrollbar
- The toolbar contains toolbar buttons
- The scroll pane contains an editor pane with a plug-in editor kit for styled text

FIGURE 55   Components Contained in a Primary Window

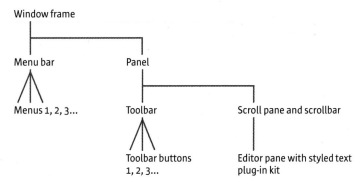

Note the appearance of the embedded containers in an actual primary window and their relationship to the underlying structure, as shown in the following figure:

FIGURE 56   Anatomy of a Primary Window

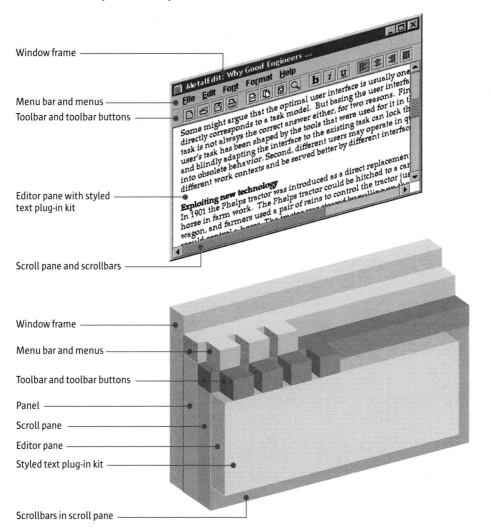

Window frame

Menu bar and menus

Toolbar and toolbar buttons

Editor pane with styled
text plug-in kit

Scroll pane and scrollbars

Window frame

Menu bar and menus

Toolbar and toolbar buttons

Panel

Scroll pane

Editor pane

Styled text plug-in kit

Scrollbars in scroll pane

Constructing Windows

Primary windows, secondary windows, utility windows, and plain windows serve as the top-level containers for all the interface elements of your application.

FIGURE 57   Top-Level Containers

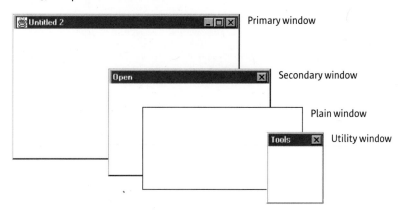

Primary windows are implemented using the JFrame component. Secondary windows and utility windows are implemented using the JDialog component. Plain windows are implemented using the JWindow component.

Primary Windows

JFC applications display information such as documents inside primary windows. Such windows are provided by the native operating system of the platform on which the application is running—for instance, UNIX, Microsoft Windows, OS/2, or Macintosh.

Specifically, you cannot alter the appearance of the window border and **title bar**, including the **window controls**, which are provided by the native operating system. Window behavior, such as resizing, dragging, minimizing, positioning, and layering, is controlled by the native operating system.

The content provided by your application, however, assumes the Java look and feel, as shown in the following illustration of a MetalEdit document window as it appears on the Microsoft Windows platform.

FIGURE 58   Primary Window on the Microsoft Windows Platform

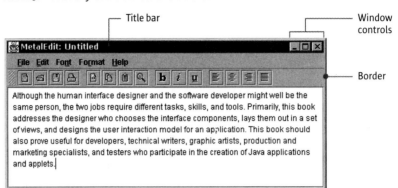

Typically, when users close or minimize a window, the operating system closes any associated secondary windows as well. However, the operating system does not take care of this behavior automatically for JFC applications.

☕ Keep track of the secondary windows in your application; close them if the primary window is closed or hide them if their primary window is minimized.

☕ Although native operating systems display a close control on the title bar of typical windows, provide a Close item or Exit item in your File menu as well.

🖿⊃ In the JFC, primary windows are created using the `JFrame` component. This component appears with the border, title bar, and window controls of the platform on which it is running. This is the JFC component you are most likely to use as the top-level container for a primary window.

Secondary Windows   Secondary windows, such as dialog boxes and alert boxes, are displayed in a window supplied by the native operating system. In the JFC, this component is called `JDialog`. It appears with the border and title bar of the platform on which it is running. Chapter 8 provides more guidelines for the design of dialog boxes and alert boxes. The following figure shows a JFC-supplied Warning alert box for the sample text-editing application, MetalEdit.

FIGURE 59   Alert Box on the Macintosh Platform

Title bar

Border

Dialog and alert box behavior, such as dragging and closing, is controlled by the native operating system. For keyboard operations that are appropriate to dialog and alert boxes, see Table 17 on page 194.

Keep in mind that some platforms do not provide close controls in the title bar for dialog boxes. Always provide a way to close the window in the dialog box or alert box itself.

The `JOptionPane` component is used to implement an alert box. If the box supplied by the JFC does not suit your needs, you can use the `JDialog` component.

Plain Windows   You can create a window that is a blank plain rectangle. The window contains no title bar or window controls, as shown in the following figure. (Note that the black border shown around this plain window is not provided by the JFC.)

FIGURE 60   Plain Window Used as the Basis for a Splash Screen

A plain window does not provide dragging, closing, minimizing, or maximizing. You can use a plain window as the container for a splash screen, which appears and disappears without user interaction, as shown in the preceding figure.

▦▭ The JWindow component is used to implement plain windows. The JFrame component is used to implement primary windows.

Utility Windows   In a non-MDI application with the Java look and feel, a utility window is often used to display a collection of tools, colors, or patterns. Unlike the palette windows provided for MDI applications, utility windows do not float above all the other windows. The following figure shows a utility window that displays a collection of tools.

FIGURE 61   Utility Window

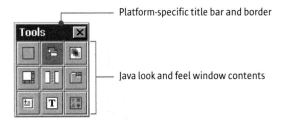

Platform-specific title bar and border

Java look and feel window contents

Unlike secondary windows, which should be closed automatically when their associated windows are closed, utility windows should not be closed when primary windows are closed.

User choices made in a utility window refer to and affect the active primary window. A utility window remains on screen for an extended period of time while users go back and forth between the utility window and primary windows. In contrast, a secondary window is designed to enable users to resolve an issue in an associated primary window and is usually dismissed once users have resolved the issue.

For information on keyboard operations appropriate for utility windows, see Table 17 on page 194.

☕ Since utility windows are not dependent on a primary window, do not automatically dismiss utility windows when primary windows are closed.

▦▭ Utility windows in your application are implemented using the JDialog component. Palettes to be used within MDI applications are implemented as a form of the JInternalFrame component.

Organizing Windows

The JFC provides a number of user interface elements you can use for the organization of windows: panels, tabbed panes, split panes, and scroll panes. Panels and panes can be used to organize windows into one or more viewing areas. A panel is a JFC component that you can use for grouping other components inside windows or other panels. A pane is a collective term for scroll panes, split panes, and tabbed panes.

FIGURE 62   Lower-Level Containers

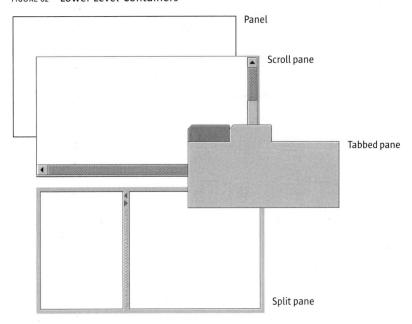

Panels

In contrast to scroll panes and tabbed panes, which typically play an interactive role in an application, a panel simply groups components within a window or another panel. Layout managers enable you to position components visually within a panel. For a thorough treatment of the visual layout and alignment of components, see "Layout and Visual Alignment" on page 47. For more information on layout managers, see *The Java Tutorial* at http://java.sun.com/docs/books/tutorial.

Scroll Panes   A **scroll pane** is a specialized container offering vertical and horizontal scrollbars that enable users to change the visible portion of the window contents.

Here is an example of a scroll pane with a vertical scrollbar. The size of the scroll box indicates the proportion of the content currently displayed.

FIGURE 63   Scroll Pane in a Document Window

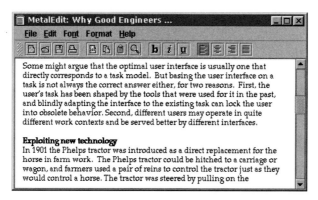

You can choose whether scrollbars are always displayed in the scroll pane or whether they appear only when needed.

☕ Unless otherwise indicated, use the default setting for horizontal scrollbars, which specifies that they appear only when needed.

☕ If the data in a list is known and appears to fit in the available space (for example, a predetermined set of colors), specify that a vertical scrollbar should appear only if needed. For instance, if users change the font, the list items might become too large to fit in the available space, and a vertical scrollbar would be required.

☕ If the data in a scroll pane sometimes requires a vertical scrollbar, specify that the vertical scrollbar always be present. Otherwise, the data must be reformatted whenever the vertical scrollbar appears or disappears.

▤⊃ Scrollbars are obtained by placing the component, such as a text area, inside a scroll pane.

Scrollbars   A **scrollbar** is a component that enables users to control what portion of a document or list (or similar information) is visible on screen. In locales with left-to-right writing systems, scrollbars appear along the bottom and the right sides of a scroll pane, a list, a combo box, a text area, or an editor pane. In locales with right-to-left writing systems, such as Hebrew and Arabic, scrollbars appear along the bottom and left sides of the relevant component.

By default, scrollbars appear only when needed to view information that is not currently visible, although you can specify that the scrollbar is always present.

The size of the **scroll box** represents the proportion of the window content that is currently visible. The position of the scroll box within the scrollbar represents the position of the visible material within the document. As users move the scroll box, the view of the document changes accordingly. If the entire document is visible, the scroll box fills the entire channel.

Both horizontal and vertical scroll boxes have a minimum size of 16 x 16 pixels so that users can still manipulate them when viewing very long documents or lists.

At either end of the scrollbar is a **scroll arrow**, which is used for controlling small movements of the data.

The following figure shows horizontal and vertical scrollbars. Each scrollbar is a rectangle consisting of a textured scroll box, a recessed channel, and scroll arrows.

FIGURE 64   Vertical and Horizontal Scrollbars

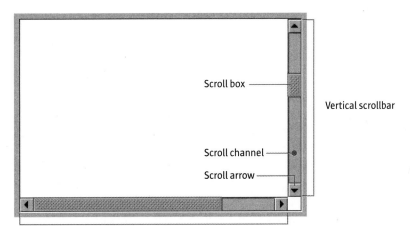

Do not confuse the scrollbar with a slider, which is used to select a value. For details on sliders, see page 159.

Users drag the scroll box, click the scroll arrows, or click in the channel to change the contents of the viewing area. When users click a scroll arrow, more of the document or list scrolls into view. The contents of the pane or list move in increments based on the type of data. When users hold down the mouse button, the pane or list scrolls continuously.

For a description of keyboard operations for scrollbars, see Table 22 on page 197.

☕ Scroll the content approximately one view at a time when users click in the scrollbar's channel. For instance, in a document, a view might represent a page of text. Leave one small unit of overlap from the previous view to provide context for the user. For instance, in scrolling through a long document, help users become oriented to the new page by providing one line of text from the previous page.

☕ Scroll the content one small unit at a time when users click a scroll arrow. (A small unit might be one line of text, one row in a table, or 10 to 20 pixels of a graphic.)

☕ Display a horizontal scrollbar if the view cannot show everything that is important—for instance, in a word-processing application that prepares printed pages, users might want to look at the margins as well as the text.

⊕ If you are using the Java 2 SDK, place scrollbars in the orientation that is suitable for the writing system of your target locale. For example, in the U.S. locale, the scrollbars appear along the right side of the scroll pane or other component. In other locales, they might appear along the left side of the scroll pane.

Tabbed Panes   A **tabbed pane** is a container that enables users to switch between several content panes (usually `JPanel` components) that appear to share the same space on screen.

The tabs themselves can contain text or images or both. A typical tabbed pane appears with tabs displayed at the top. Alternatively, the tabs can be displayed on one of the other three sides. If the tabs cannot fit in a single row, additional rows are created automatically. Note that tabs do not change position when they are selected. For the first row of tabs, there is no separator line between the selected tab and the pane.

The following figure shows the initial content pane in the JFC-supplied color chooser. Note that the tabbed pane is displayed within a dialog box that uses the borders, title bar, and window controls of the platform on which its associated application is running.

FIGURE 65   Swatches Content Pane in the JFC Color Chooser

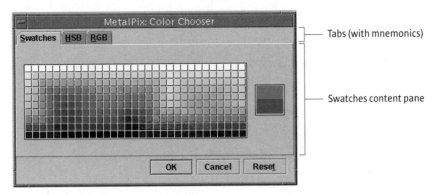

Users choose which content pane to view by clicking the corresponding tab. The content pane changes accordingly, as shown in the following figure of the content pane associated with the third tab in the color chooser.

For a list of keyboard operations appropriate for tabbed panes, see Table 25 on page 198.

FIGURE 66   RGB Content Pane in the JFC Color Chooser

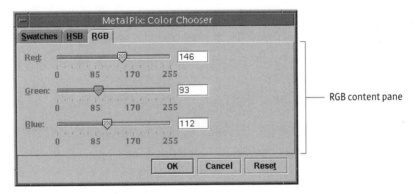

You can use tabbed panes to good advantage in dialog boxes, such as a preferences dialog box, that require you to fit a lot of information into a small area.

You can also use tabbed panes to provide a way for users to switch between content panes that represent:

■ Different ways to view the same information, like a color chooser's RGB and HSB panes

■ Different parts of an informational unit, like worksheets that are part of a workbook in a spreadsheet application

☕ Use headline capitalization for tab names.

☕ Provide mnemonics so users can navigate from tab to tab and from tabs to associated content panes using keyboard operations.

☕ Do not nest tabbed panes.

☕ If your tabbed pane requires multiple rows of tabs, consider dividing the content among several dialog boxes or components. Multiple rows of tabs can be confusing.

Split Panes A **split pane** is a container that divides a pane into resizable panes. Split panes enable users to adjust the relative sizes of two adjacent panes. The Java look and feel drag texture (along with a pointer change) indicates that users can resize split panes.

To adjust the size of the split panes, users drag the splitter bar, as shown in the following figure.

FIGURE 67   Split Pane (Horizontal Orientation)

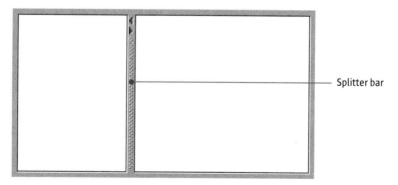

Splitter bar

Users can also control the splitter bar by clicking one of the optional zoom buttons shown in the following figure. Clicking a button moves the splitter bar to its extreme upper or lower position. If the splitter bar is already at its extreme, clicking restores the panes to the size they were before the zoom operation (or before the user dragged the splitter bar to close one of the panes).

For a list of keyboard operations appropriate for split panes, see Table 24 on page 198.

FIGURE 68 Zoom Buttons in a Split Pane (Vertical Orientation)

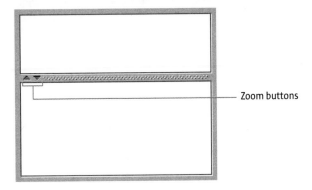

Zoom buttons

Include zoom buttons in split panes because they are very convenient for users.

Nested Split Panes In addition to splitting panes either horizontally or vertically, you can nest one split pane inside another. The following figure portrays a mail application in which the top pane of a vertically split pane has another split pane embedded in it.

FIGURE 69   Nested Split Panes

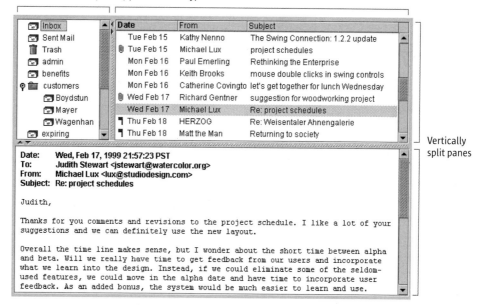

Working With Multiple Document Interfaces   A multiple
document interface (MDI) provides a way to manage multiple windows that
are confined inside a main window. A limitation to using the MDI application
model is that users cannot drag the application's windows outside the main
window. To support MDI designers, the JFC provides the internal frame and
palette window.

⊞⊏◠   If you are working with an MDI using the Java look and feel, the
JDialog component can be used to create secondary windows.

Internal Frames   To get standard window features in an MDI, you must put an
internal frame inside the desktop pane. A **desktop pane** is a component
placed inside a window that holds internal frames for an MDI application.

The internal frame is a **container** used in MDI applications to create windows
that users cannot drag outside of the desktop pane. In an MDI application
that uses the Java look and feel, internal frames have a window border, title
bar, and standard window controls with the Java look and feel. However, the
window that contains the desktop pane is a native platform window with the
native look and feel, as shown in the following figure.

FIGURE 70   Internal Frames in an MDI Application

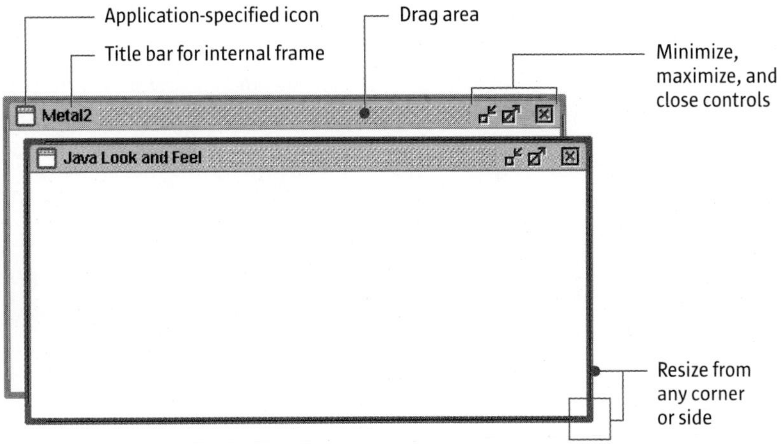

Application-specified icon ——   — Drag area

Title bar for internal frame ——   — Minimize,
maximize, and
close controls

Metal2   ⌐ ⌐ ⌐

Java Look and Feel   ⌐ ⌐ ⌐

— Resize from
any corner
or side

Users can use the mouse to:

- Activate a window (and deactivate the previously activated window) by clicking anywhere in the window

- Adjust the size of a resizable internal frame by dragging from any side or corner

- Drag the internal frame by the title bar within the desktop pane

- Minimize, maximize, restore, and close the internal frame by clicking the appropriate window controls

For keyboard operations appropriate to internal frames, see Table 16 on page 193.

A **minimized internal frame** is a horizontally oriented component (shown in the following figure) that represents an internal frame that has been minimized. The width of these minimized internal frames is sized to accommodate the window title. Minimized internal frames consist of a drag area followed by an area containing an application-specific icon and text, which displays the name of the internal frame.

FIGURE 71   Minimized Internal Frame

— Drag area   — Text

Users can rearrange minimized internal frames by dragging the textured area. Users can click the icon and text area in a minimized internal frame to restore the frame to its previous location and size.

For details on the keyboard operations appropriate for minimized internal frames, see Table 16 on page 193.

Palettes

A **palette window** is a type of internal frame that can float above other internal frames within the desktop pane for an MDI application. The close control is optional.

The following figure shows a palette window from a hypothetical graphical interface builder with a set of buttons that lets users construct menus.

FIGURE 72   Palette Window

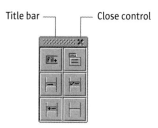

Title bar ———   ——— Close control

Palette windows often contain toggle buttons; users can click the toggle buttons to select them. However, palette windows can contain any component. Users can close palette windows (if you provide a close control), but they cannot resize, minimize, or maximize them.

For keyboard operations for palette windows, see Table 16 on page 193.

If you are writing a non-MDI application, use utility windows instead of palette windows so that the user can drag them anywhere on the screen.

A palette window is a specific style of `JInternalFrame` and, therefore, can be used only within a desktop pane. Use the client properties mechanism to set the `JInternalFrame.isPalette` to true.

8: DIALOG BOXES

A **dialog box** is a temporary, secondary window in which users perform a task that is supplemental to the task in the primary window. For example, a dialog box might enable users to set preferences or choose a file from the hard disk. A dialog box can contain panes and panels, text, graphics, controls (such as checkboxes, radio buttons, or sliders), and one or more command buttons. Dialog boxes use the native window frame of the platform on which they are running.

An **alert box** is a dialog box that provides for brief interaction with users. Alert boxes present error messages, warn of potentially harmful actions, obtain information from users, and display informational messages. The basic alert box has a symbol that identifies the type of the alert, a textual message, and one or more command buttons. The layout of these components is supplied by the Java look and feel.

FIGURE 73   Dialog Box and Alert Box

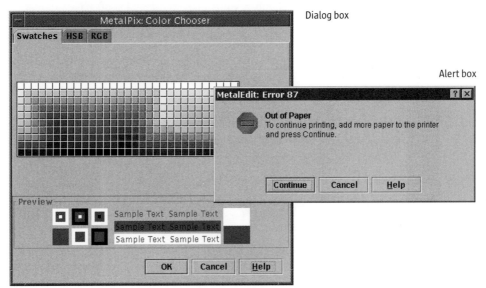

☕ If your application is based on a multiple document interface (MDI), use the dialog boxes and alert boxes presented in this chapter. Because these secondary windows use the platform's native windows (and not the JFC-supplied internal frame), they are free to move outside the desktop pane.

Modal and Modeless Dialog Boxes
Dialog boxes can be modal or modeless. A **modal dialog box** prevents users from interacting with the application until the dialog box is dismissed. However, users can move a modal dialog box and interact with other applications while the modal dialog box is open. This behavior is sometimes called "application-modal."

A **modeless dialog box** does not prevent users from interacting with the application they are in or with any other application. Users can go back and forth between a modeless dialog box and other application windows.

☕ Use modeless dialog boxes whenever possible. The order in which users perform tasks might vary, or users might want to check information in other windows before dismissing the dialog box. Users might also want to go back and forth between the dialog box and the primary window.

☕ Use modal dialog boxes when interaction with the application cannot proceed while the dialog box is displayed. For example, a progress dialog box that appears while your application is loading its data should be a modal dialog box.

Dialog Box Design
The following figure illustrates dialog box design guidelines for the Java look and feel. The dialog box has a title in the window's title bar, a series of user interface elements, and a row of command buttons. The default command button is the OK button, indicated by its heavy border. The underlined letters are mnemonics, which remind users how to activate components by pressing the Alt key and the appropriate character key. The noneditable Ruler Units combo box has initial keyboard focus, indicating that the user's next keystrokes will take effect in that component.

FIGURE 74 Sample Dialog Box

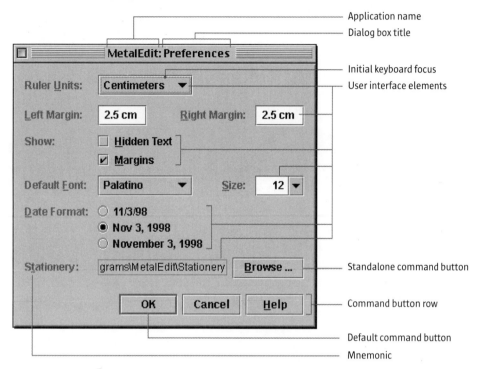

☕ Use the form "Application Name: Title" for the title of the dialog box (which is displayed in the title bar).

☕ Include mnemonics for all user interface elements except the default button and the Cancel button.

☕ When opening a dialog box, provide initial keyboard focus to the component that you expect users to operate first. This focus is especially important for users who must use a keyboard to navigate your application (for example, users with visual and mobility impairments).

⊕ Consider the effect of internationalization on your design. Use a layout manager, which allows for text strings to become bigger or smaller when translated to another language.

For more information on internationalization, see "Planning for Internationalization and Localization" on page 33. For details on keyboard support for navigating through dialog boxes, see Table 17 on page 194. For information on how to capitalize text in dialog boxes, see "Capitalization of Text in the Interface" on page 46.

Tab Traversal Order   The tab traversal order is the order in which the components in the dialog box receive keyboard focus on successive presses of the Tab key. If users press the Tab key when keyboard focus is on the last component in the dialog box, you should return keyboard focus to the first component. The following figure shows the tab traversal order that the designer has set for this preferences dialog box.

FIGURE 75   Tab Traversal Order in the Sample Dialog Box

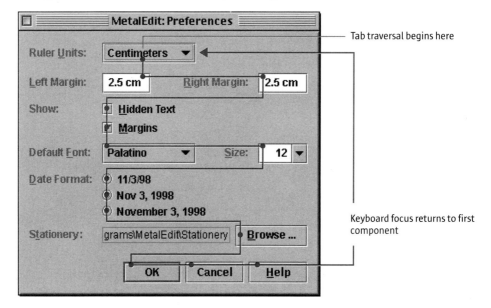

Specify a logical tab traversal order for the user interface elements. The traversal order should match the reading order for your application's specified locale. For example, in English, the traversal order is left to right, top to bottom. By default, the traversal order is the sequence in which you added the components to the dialog box.

The setNextFocusableComponent method from JComponent can be used to specify the next component to receive keyboard focus.

Spacing in Dialog Boxes   The following figure shows the spacing you must provide between the borders of the dialog box and the components in the dialog box.

FIGURE 76   Spacing Between the Border and Components of a Dialog Box

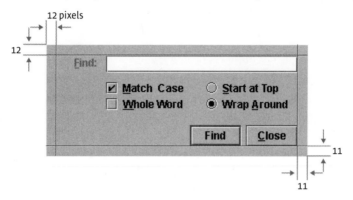

 Include 12 pixels between the top and left borders of the dialog box and its components. Include 11 pixels between the bottom and right borders of the dialog box and its components. (To the eye, the 11-pixel spacing appears to be 12 pixels because the white borders on the lower and right edges of the components are not visually significant.)

See "Design Grids" on page 49 for a general description of how to place text and components in a dialog box.

Command Buttons in Dialog Boxes   In dialog boxes, you can place command buttons alone or in a command button row at the bottom of the dialog box, as shown in Figure 74 on page 113. The most common command buttons that you might use in a command button row are the Help, Close, OK, Cancel, Apply, and Reset buttons. If you use other command buttons, make sure their labels describe the action they perform.

 Place command buttons that apply to the dialog box as a whole in the command button row at the bottom of the dialog box. This includes all buttons that dismiss the dialog box as one of their actions.

 Align buttons in the command button row along the lower-right edge of the dialog box. (The alignment of the command button row in JFC-supplied alert boxes is different from the alignment in dialog boxes.)

For consistency in the look and spacing of command buttons, follow the guidelines on "Command Buttons" on page 148. For keyboard operations appropriate to command buttons, see Table 15 on page 193.

Help Buttons   You can use a Help button in any dialog box. A Help button enables users to obtain additional information about the dialog box. For example, when users click Help in the Error alert box on page 125, the application opens a window with additional information on the cause of the error.

☕ When users click the Help button, open a secondary or utility window that displays the help information.

☕ Place the Help button last in a group of command buttons. For languages that read from left to right, the Help button should be the rightmost button.

Close Buttons   The Close button is commonly used to dismiss simple dialog boxes, such as an Info alert box. The Close button is also commonly used to dismiss dialog boxes in which user actions take effect immediately. In these dialog boxes, users do not need to press an OK button for the settings to take effect. A Close button is appropriate in both modal and modeless dialog boxes.

The following dialog box, which contains a schedule reminder, includes a Close button that users can click to dismiss the dialog box.

FIGURE 77   Dialog Box With a Close Button

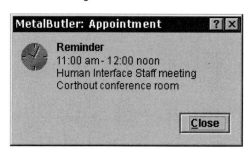

☕ When users click the Close button, dismiss the dialog box and do not make additional changes to the system.

OK and Cancel Buttons   The OK and Cancel buttons work well in dialog boxes in which users specify options or settings. OK enables users to save the settings, whereas Cancel enables users to ignore any changed settings. In most cases, OK is the default button. OK and Cancel are appropriate in both modal and modeless dialog boxes. The following figure shows a preferences dialog box with OK, Cancel, and Help buttons.

FIGURE 78   Dialog Box With OK, Cancel, and Help Buttons

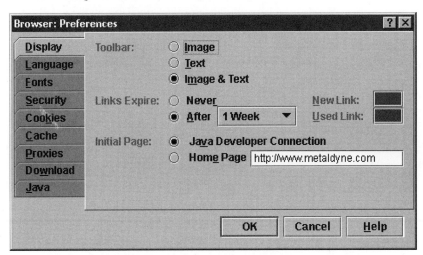

When users click the OK button, save the settings or carry out the commands specified in the dialog box and close the dialog box. Whenever possible, use a command name that describes the action (such as Print or Find) instead of OK.

When users click the Cancel button, close the dialog box and restore the settings in the dialog box to the state they were in when the dialog box was opened.

Activate the Cancel button when users press the Escape key. The Cancel button does not need keyboard focus for this interaction; only the dialog box must have focus. The Cancel button and its keyboard equivalent are not built into the JFC; you must implement them yourself.

Do not add a mnemonic to the Cancel button.

Do not use the Cancel button in a dialog box where settings become persistent before the dialog box is closed (for example, in a dialog box that has an Apply button). Users might be confused about whether the changes will be undone when they press Cancel. In dialog boxes where you want users to be able to view changes without committing to them, use Preview, OK, and Cancel buttons. Use Preview to show the effects of the changes in the document window without dismissing the dialog box. Use OK to make the changes persistent, and use Cancel to undo the changes. OK and Cancel should dismiss the dialog box as usual.

Apply and Reset Buttons   The Apply and Reset buttons work well in dialog boxes that remain open for repeated use, as shown in the properties dialog box in the following figure. Apply and Reset often appear together in modeless dialog boxes.

FIGURE 79   Dialog Box With Apply, Reset, and Close Buttons

☕ Use the Apply button to carry out the changes users specify in the dialog box without closing the dialog box.

☕ Use the Reset button to restore the values in the dialog box to the values specified by the last Apply command. If users have not activated Apply, restore the values in effect when the dialog box was opened. Do not close the dialog box when users choose Reset.

☕ If you include the Close button in a dialog box with Apply and Reset buttons, make Close dismiss the dialog box without applying changes.

Default Command Buttons   The default command button is the button that the application activates when users press Enter or Return. The JFC gives the default command button a heavier border than other command buttons. In most cases, you should assign the default button the action that users are most likely to perform, as shown with the OK button in the following figure. The default button does not need to have keyboard focus when users press Enter or Return.

FIGURE 80   Dialog Box With a Default Command Button

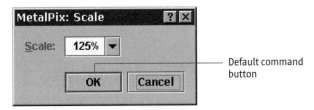

Default command
button

In cases where keyboard focus is on a component that accepts the Enter or Return key, such as a multiline text area, the default button is not activated when users press the key. Instead, the insertion point moves to the beginning of a new line. To operate the default button, users must move focus to a component that does not accept Enter or Return.

If the dialog box has a default button, make it the first command button in the group. For example, in languages that read from left to right, the default button is the leftmost button.

Do not add a mnemonic for the default command button.

You are not required to have a default command button in every dialog box and alert box. A command that might cause users to lose data should never be the default button, even if it is the action that users are most likely to perform. The following alert box asks users if they want to replace an existing file. The alert box has Replace and Cancel buttons, neither of which is the default command button.

FIGURE 81   Alert Box Without a Default Button

Common Dialog Boxes

The find, login, preferences, print, and progress dialog boxes are common in many applications. These dialog boxes are not supplied by the Java Foundation Classes. The following sections show simple versions of these dialog boxes that are consistent with the Java look and feel. You can adapt the designs for these dialog boxes to suit your needs.

Find Dialog Boxes

A find dialog box enables users to search for a specified text string. In most cases, you should make this dialog box modeless. An example is shown in the following figure.

FIGURE 82   Sample Find Dialog Box

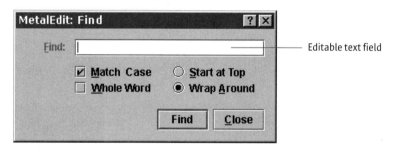

Editable text field

Login Dialog Boxes

A login dialog box (shown in the following figure) enables users to identify themselves and enter a password. Depending on where you use this dialog box in your application, you can make it modal or modeless.

FIGURE 83   Sample Login Dialog Box

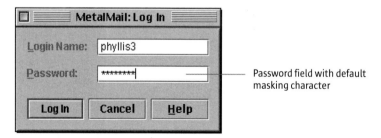

Password field with default masking character

Preferences Dialog Boxes

A preferences dialog box (shown in the following figure) enables users to view and modify the characteristics of an application. In most cases, you should make this dialog box modeless.

FIGURE 84   Sample Preferences Dialog Box

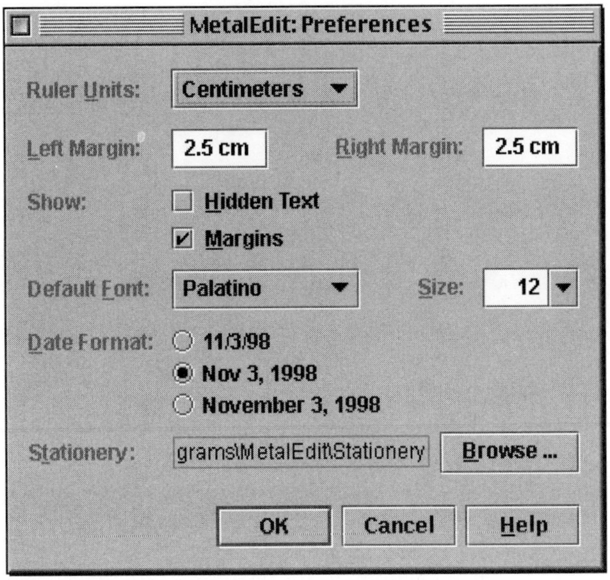

If your preferences dialog box is very complex, you can simplify it by using a tabbed pane to organize the options, as shown in Figure 78 on page 117.

Print Dialog Boxes   A print dialog box enables users to print and to specify print settings (such as the number of copies).

☕ Use the print dialog box available from the AWT. On Microsoft Windows and Macintosh platforms, the AWT uses the native print dialog box. For other environments, the AWT uses the print dialog box supplied with the JDK.

Progress Dialog Boxes   A progress dialog box provides feedback for long operations and lets users know that the system is working on the previous command. The following progress dialog box monitors the progress of a file copy operation. The dialog box includes the JFC progress bar, a command button that users can click to stop the process, and labels to further explain the progress of the operation. In most cases, you should make a progress dialog box modeless.

FIGURE 85   Sample Progress Dialog Box

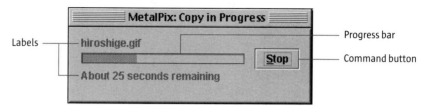

Display a progress dialog box (or supply a progress bar elsewhere in your application) if an operation takes longer than two seconds.

If you include a button to stop the process, place it after the progress bar. (In languages that read from left to right, the button appears to the right of the progress bar.) If the state will remain as it was before the process started, use a Cancel button. If the process might alter the state as it progresses (for example, deleted records will not be restored), use a Stop button. If stopping the process could lead to data loss, give users a chance to confirm the Stop command by displaying a Warning alert box.

Close the progress dialog box automatically when the operation is complete.

If delays are a common occurrence in your application (for example, in a web browser), build a progress bar into the primary window so that you don't have to keep displaying a progress dialog box.

Because translation of the word "Stop" can result in words with subtly different meanings, point out to your translators the specialized meaning of the Stop button in a progress dialog box. Stop indicates that the process might leave the system in an altered state.

Alert Boxes

An alert box, which conveys a message or warning to users, provides an easy way for you to create a dialog box. The JFC provides four types of alert boxes: Info, Warning, Error, and Question. Each alert box is provided with a symbol that indicates its type. You provide the title, the message, and the command buttons and their labels.

The layout of an alert box is provided in the JFC, so you don't have to worry about the spacing and alignment of the message, symbol, and command buttons. If you provide additional components, such as a text field, follow the layout guidelines for that component. You can make an alert box modal or modeless.

FIGURE 86   Standard Components in an Alert Box

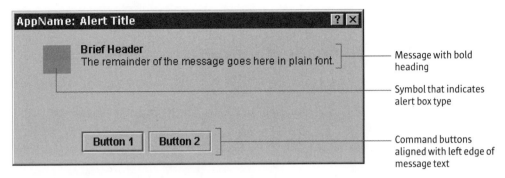

> ☕ In an alert box, begin your message with a brief heading in boldface. Start the body of the message on a separate line.

> ▤▭ In the message for an alert box, the <B>...</B> tags can be used to render a heading in boldface. The <BR> tag can be used to create a line break between the heading and the message body.

> ▤▭ An alert box is created using the JOptionPane component.

Info Alert Boxes   An Info alert box presents general information to users. The symbol in the Info alert box is a blue circle with the letter i. The following Info alert box from an encyclopedia application provides information about a sponge.

FIGURE 87   Info Alert Box

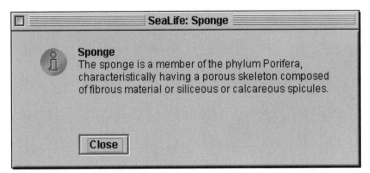

> ☕ Provide a Close button to dismiss the Info alert box. Provide additional command buttons, such as a Help button, if needed.

Warning Alert Boxes   A Warning alert box warns users about the possible consequences of an action and asks users for a response. The symbol in the Warning alert box is a yellow triangle with an exclamation point. The following alert box warns users that a file save operation will replace an existing file.

FIGURE 88   Warning Alert Box

☕ Keep the message in the Warning alert box brief, and use terms that are familiar to users.

☕ Include at least two buttons in a Warning alert box: one button to perform the action and the other to cancel the action. Provide the command buttons with labels that describe the action they perform.

☕ If appropriate, provide a Help button that opens a secondary or utility window that gives background information about the warning. Do not close the alert box when users click the Help button.

☕ Do not make a command button whose action might cause loss of data the default button. Users might press the Enter or Return key without reading the message. In such a case, you might not provide a default button.

Error Alert Boxes   An Error alert box reports system and application errors to users. The symbol in the Error alert box is a red octagon with a rectangle. The following Error alert box reports that a printer is out of paper and provides users with three options. Clicking the Continue button resumes printing and dismisses the alert box. Clicking the Cancel button terminates the print job and dismisses the alert box. Clicking the Help button opens a secondary window that gives background information about the error.

FIGURE 89   Error Alert Box

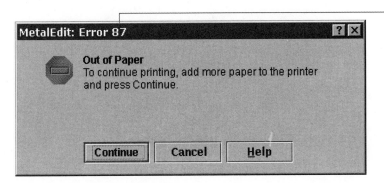

Error number
in title

☕ Include an error number in the title bar of an Error alert box. The error number is helpful for users in obtaining technical assistance, especially if the error message is localized in a language not spoken by the technical support personnel.

☕ In the message of an Error alert box, explain what happened, the cause of the problem, and what the user can do about it. Keep the message brief and use terms that are familiar to users.

☕ If appropriate, provide a Help button to open a separate online help window that gives background information about the error. Do not close the alert box when users click the Help button.

☕ If possible, provide buttons or other controls to resolve the error noted in the Error alert box. Label the buttons according to the action they perform. If users cannot resolve the error from the alert box, provide a Close button.

Question Alert Boxes   A Question alert box requests information from users. You can add components to this alert box (for example, a text field, list, or combo box) in which users can type a value or make a selection. The layout of the standard components (the symbol, message, and command buttons) is provided by the JFC. If you add components, follow the layout guidelines for that component. The symbol in the Question alert box is a green rectangle with a question mark.

The following Question alert box includes a label and text field in addition to the standard components.

FIGURE 90   Question Alert Box

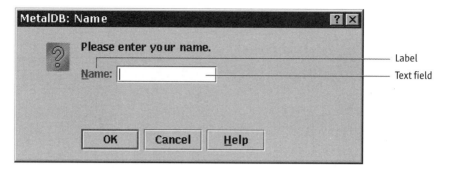

Label

Text field

When you add components to a Question alert box, align them with the leading edge of the message. For languages that read from left to right, the leading edge is the left edge.

Color Choosers

A **color chooser** provides one or more content panes from which users can select colors and a preview panel from which users can view the selected colors in context. You can display a color chooser in a dialog box, as shown in the following figure. The three command buttons (OK, Cancel, and Help) are part of the dialog box, not the color chooser.

FIGURE 91   Standard Color Chooser

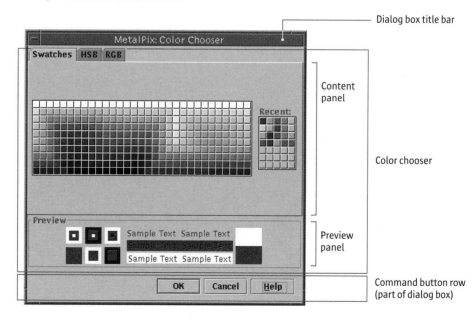

Dialog box title bar

Content panel

Color chooser

Preview panel

Command button row (part of dialog box)

As supplied by the JFC, the color chooser offers users three methods for selecting a color:

- **Swatches**. Users can select a color from a palette (as shown in the preceding figure).

- **HSB**. Users can choose the hue, saturation, and brightness values for a color.

- **RGB**. Users can choose the red, green, and blue values for a color.

If your application requires a different method for choosing colors, you can add a content pane with that feature. You can also remove existing content panes. If you use only one content pane, the tab disappears. In addition, you can specify your own preview panel.

▤▷ The color chooser is a panel. The color panel can be inserted in a dialog box by using the `JDialog` container.

9: MENUS AND TOOLBARS

A **menu** displays a list of choices (menu items) for users to choose or browse through. Typically, menus are logically grouped and displayed by an application so that a user need not memorize all available commands or options. Menus in the Java look and feel are "sticky"—that is, they remain posted on screen after users click the menu title. Usually the primary means to access your application's features, menus also provide a quick way for users to see what those features are.

A **toolbar** is a collection of frequently used commands or options that appear as a row of toolbar buttons. Toolbars normally appear horizontally beneath a primary window's menu bar, but they can be dragged anywhere in the window or into a separate window. Toolbars typically contain buttons, but you can provide other components (such as text fields and combo boxes) as well.

In Java look and feel applications, you can provide three kinds of menus: drop-down menus, submenus, and contextual menus. A **drop-down menu** is a menu whose titles appear in the menu bar. A **submenu** appears adjacent to a menu item in a drop-down menu; its presence is indicated by an arrow next to the item. A **contextual menu** displays lists of commands, settings, or attributes that apply to the item or selected items under the pointer.

FIGURE 92   Drop-down Menu, Submenu, Contextual Menu, and Toolbar

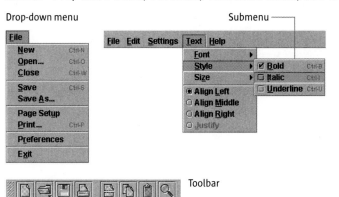

Toolbar

Menu Elements

In the Java look and feel, menus use a highlight color (primary 2) for the background of selected menu titles and menu items. The following figure shows an example of a drop-down menu that is selected and displayed. Within the Text menu, the Style item is selected; a submenu appears that includes the Bold, Italic, and Underline checkbox menu items. (The Italic checkbox menu item is highlighted.)

A separator divides the menu items for specifying font, style, and size from the alignment radio button items. Keyboard shortcuts appear to the right of the frequently used menu items, and mnemonics are included for each menu title and menu item.

FIGURE 93   Menu Elements

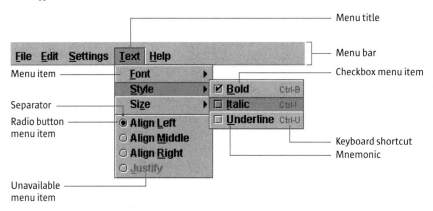

Menu Bars

The **menu bar** appears at the top of a primary window and contains menu titles, which describe the content of each menu. Menu titles usually appear as text; however, it is possible to use a graphic or a graphic with text as a menu title. Menu titles in the Java look and feel contain mnemonics only if they are explicitly set by the developer. See "Mnemonics" on page 88 for details.

A drop-down menu appears when users choose a menu title in the menu bar.

☕ If the primary window has a menu bar, display it as a single line across the top of the window.

☕ Do not display menu bars in secondary windows unless you have a compelling reason to do so (such as a complex set of activities in the secondary window).

☕ Be sure to include mnemonics for every menu title in your menu bar.

If your applet runs in the user's current browser window (with the browser menu bar), do not display your own menu bar in the applet. Although applets displayed inside a browser window can theoretically have their own menu bars, users are often confused when both the browser window and the applet have menu bars. If your applet requires a menu bar, display the applet in a separate browser window without its own menu bar or navigation controls.

Even on Macintosh systems, which ordinarily place a menu bar only at the top of the screen, display menu bars in windows for a Java look and feel application. On the Macintosh, the screen-top menu bar remains, but, since all the application menus are in the windows, the only command in the screen-top menu bar should be Quit in the File menu.

Drop-down Menus   The menu bar contains all of the drop-down menus and submenus in your application. Each menu in the menu bar is represented by its menu title. The titles describe the content of each menu. (The title for a submenu is its menu item in the drop-down menu.)

Users can display menus in two ways:

- To post a menu (that is, to display it and have it stay up until the next click even though the mouse button has been released), users click the menu title. Users can then move the pointer over other menu titles to view other menus.

- To pull down a menu, users press the mouse button over the menu title. The menu title is highlighted, and the menu drops down. When users choose a command and release the mouse button, the menu closes.

For details on keyboard navigation, selection, and activation in menus, see Table 20 on page 196.

Use single words for your menu titles.

Use menu titles that help users guess which menu contains the item of particular interest at a given moment. For example, the Edit menu typically contains commands that enable users to change or edit the contents of their documents or data.

Include mnemonics in all your menu titles.

Submenus   A submenu is a menu that users open by highlighting a menu item in a higher-level menu. Sometimes you can shorten a menu by moving related choices to a submenu. Submenus (such as the Style submenu shown in the following figure) appear adjacent to the submenu indicator. For instance, the Style item opens a submenu consisting of three items: Bold, Italic, and Underline. Note that the items in the Style submenu include both keyboard shortcuts and mnemonics.

Users display submenus by clicking or by dragging over the corresponding menu item. The first item in the submenu aligns with the submenu indicator, slightly overlapping the main menu. Just as in other menus, items in the submenu are highlighted when the user moves the pointer over them.

For a list of keyboard operations in submenus, see Table 20 on page 196.

FIGURE 94   Menu Item With Its Submenu

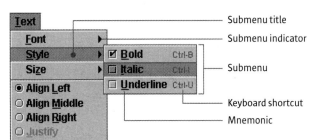

Since many people find submenus difficult to use, avoid the use of a second level of submenus. If you want to present a large or complex set of choices, display them in a dialog box.

Submenus are created using the JMenu component.

Menu Items   A simple **menu item** consists of the command name, such as Undo. When a menu item is available for use, its text is displayed in black, as shown in the following figure.

FIGURE 95   Typical Menu Items

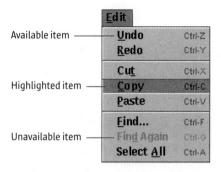

When users position the pointer over an individual item within a menu, the menu item (if available) is highlighted.

Users can choose menu items in two ways:

- In a posted menu, users click a menu item to choose it and close the menu.

- In a pulled-down menu, users drag over a menu item to highlight it. Releasing the mouse button chooses the command and closes the menu.

For a list of keyboard operations for menu items, see Table 20 on page 196.

Available and Unavailable Items   Here are some guidelines for handling available and unavailable menu items in your application.

☕ If an application feature is not currently available in a window, but users can do something to make it available, make the corresponding menu item unavailable and dim its text. For example, the Undo command might not be available until the user has made a change in a document window.

☕ If all the items in a menu are unavailable, do not make the menu unavailable. In this way, users can still display the menu and view all its (inactive) items. Similarly, if all the items in a submenu are currently not available, do not make the original menu item unavailable.

☕ If there is nothing users can do to make a menu item available, omit the item entirely rather than just making it unavailable. Making an item unavailable implies that users can do something to make the item available. A similar rule applies to submenu items and contextual menus.

Composition and Construction of Items   Here are some recommendations for the use of concise language, consistent capitalization, and keyboard operations in menu items.

☕ Make your menu items brief, and confine them to a single line.

☕ Use headline capitalization in menu titles and menu items.

☕ Include mnemonics for all menu items.

☕ Offer keyboard shortcuts for frequently used menu items.

☕ Use the same keyboard shortcut if a menu item appears in several menus—for instance, if a Cut item appears in a contextual menu as well as in a drop-down Edit menu, use Ctrl-X for both.

Commonly used keyboard shortcuts are described in "Typical File Menu" on page 137, "Typical Edit Menu" on page 138, and "Typical Help Menu" on page 139.

Ellipses in Items   Ellipses (...) are punctuation marks that indicate the omission of one or more words that must be supplied in order to make a construction complete. In your menus, you can use ellipses in a similar way: to indicate that the command issued by a menu item needs more specification in order to make it complete.

☕ If a menu item does not fully specify a command and users need a dialog box to finish the specification, use an ellipsis after the menu item. For example, after choosing Save As..., users are presented with a file chooser to specify a file name and location.

☕ Do not use an ellipsis mark simply to indicate that a secondary or utility window will appear. For example, choosing Preferences displays a dialog box; because that display is the entire effect of the command, however, Preferences is not followed by an ellipsis.

Organization of Items   You can group menu items with separators or, in the case of lengthy extensible menus, with a grid layout. Here are the guidelines:

☕ Use separators to group similar menu items in a way that helps users find items and better understand their range of choices. For instance, in a typical File menu, the commands that affect saving are separated from those that are relevant to printing.

▦▷ If a menu is or has the potential to become very long (for instance, in menus that present lists of bookmarks or email recipients), a grid layout should be used to display the menu choices in multiple columns.

Checkbox Menu Items   A **checkbox menu item** is a menu item that appears with a checkbox next to it to represent an on or off setting. A check mark in the adjacent checkbox graphic indicates that the value associated with that menu item is selected. A dimmed checkbox menu item shows a gray box (checked or unchecked) that indicates that the setting cannot be changed. The following figure shows checked, unchecked, and unavailable menu items.

FIGURE 96   Checkbox Menu Items

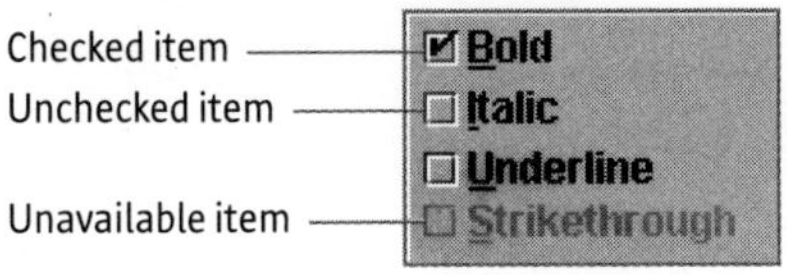

Checked item ————— ☑ **Bold**
Unchecked item ————— ☐ **Italic**
                                    ☐ **Underline**
Unavailable item ————— ☐ Strikethrough

You can use checkbox menu items to present users with a nonexclusive choice.

For a list of keyboard operations for checkbox menu items, see Table 20 on page 196.

☕ For consistency, use the standard checkbox graphic for checkbox menu items.

☕ As with all menu items, after users choose a checkbox menu item, the menu is dismissed. To choose another item, users must reopen the menu. Therefore, use checkbox menu items with restraint. If users must set more than one or two related preferences, place the checkboxes in a dialog box (or provide a palette or toolbar buttons for the preferences).

Radio Button Menu Items   A **radio button menu item** is a menu item that appears with a radio button next to it to represent an off or on setting. Each radio button menu item offers users a single choice within a set of radio button menu items, as illustrated in the following set of alignment options.

FIGURE 97   Radio Button Menu Items

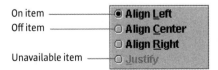

On item ————— ◉ **Align Left**
Off item ————— ○ **Align Center**
                             ○ **Align Right**
Unavailable item ————— ○ Justify

For a list of keyboard operations for radio button menu items, see Table 20 on page 196.

 To indicate that the radio button items are part of a set, group them and use separators to distinguish them from other menu items.

 As with all menu items, after users choose a radio button menu item, the menu is dismissed. To choose another item, users must reopen the menu. Therefore, use radio button menu items with restraint. If users must set more than one or two related preferences, place the radio buttons in a dialog box (or provide a palette or toolbar buttons for the preferences).

Separators   A **separator** is a line graphic that is used to divide menu items into logical groupings, as shown in the following figure.

FIGURE 98   Separators in a Menu

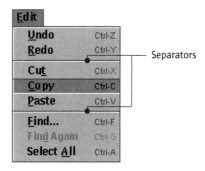

Users can never choose a separator.

You can use separators to make lengthy menus easier to read.

 While separators serve important functions on menus, avoid using them elsewhere in your application. Instead, use blank space or an occasional titled border to delineate areas in dialog boxes or other components.

Common Menus   Several drop-down menus, such as File, Edit, and Help, occur in many applications. These menus are not supplied by the Java Foundation Classes. The following sections show simple versions of these menus that are consistent with the Java look and feel. You can adapt these menus to suit your needs.

 If your application needs these commonly used menus, place the menu titles in this order: File, Object, Edit, Format, View, and Help. If needed, insert other menus between the View and Help menus.

Typical File Menu   The first menu displays commands that apply to an entire document or the application as a whole. Typically, this is called the File menu, but in some cases another title might be more appropriate. The following figure illustrates common File menu items in order, with mnemonics and keyboard shortcuts.

You can add or remove menu items as needed.

FIGURE 99   Typical File Menu

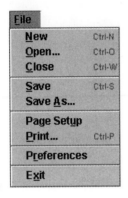

⌣ Place commands that apply to the document (or another object) or application as a whole in the File menu.

⌣ If your application manipulates objects that your users might not think of as "files," give the first menu another name. Ensure that the name corresponds to the type of object or procedure represented by the entire window in your application. For example, a project management application could have Project as its first menu, or a mail application could have a Mailbox menu.

⌣ Since the Close item dismisses the active window, close any dependent windows at the same time.

⌣ If you provide an Exit item, have it close all associated windows and terminate the application. (Be sure to use the term Exit, not Quit.)

Object Menu   Object menu items provide actions that users can perform on an object or objects. An object might be almost anything—for instance, an icon representing a person for whom you want to add an email alias.

Typical Edit Menu   The Edit menu displays items that enable users to change or edit the contents of their documents or other data. These items give users typical text-editing features. The following figure shows common Edit menu items in order, with mnemonics and keyboard shortcuts.

FIGURE 100   Typical Edit Menu

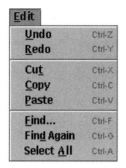

☕ Place commands that modify the contents of documents or other data in the Edit menu, including Undo, Redo, Cut, Copy, Paste, and Find.

▤▷ The Swing Undo package can be used to provide the Undo and Redo commands.

Typical Format Menu   The Format menu displays items that enable users to change such formatting elements in their documents as font, size, styles, characters, and paragraphs. The following figure shows common Format menu items with their mnemonics.

FIGURE 101   Typical Format Menu

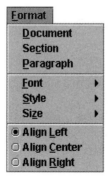

View Menu   View menu items provide ways for users to adjust the view of data in the active window. For instance, the View menu in a network management application might have items that enable users to view large or small icons for network objects.

Typical Help Menu   Help menu items provide access to online information about the features of an application. This menu also provides access to the application's About box, which displays basic information about the application. For details, see "Designing About Boxes" on page 76. The following figure shows common Help menu items (in the typical order) with their mnemonics.

These menu items will vary according to the needs of your application.

FIGURE 102   Typical Help Menu

☕ In your Help menu, allow access to online information about the features of the application.

☕ Place a separator before an About Application item that displays a dialog box with the product name, version number, company logo, product logo, legal notices, and names of contributors to the product.

⊟⊃ JavaHelp™, a standard extension to the Java Development Kit and the Java 2 SDK, can be used to build a help system for your applications.

Contextual Menus   Sometimes called a "pop-up menu," a contextual menu offers only menu items that are applicable or relevant to the object or region at the location of the pointer. The appearance of contextual menus in the Java look and feel is similar to that of drop-down menus, including the display of mnemonics and keyboard shortcuts. Contextual menus do not have a menu title. The following figure shows a contextual menu offering editing commands.

FIGURE 103 Contextual Menu

Users can display a contextual menu by clicking or pressing mouse button 2 while the pointer is over an object or area that is associated with that menu. (On the Macintosh platform, users click while holding down the Control key.)

For keyboard operations appropriate to contextual menus, see Table 20 on page 196.

☕ Ensure that any features you present in contextual menus are also available in more visible and accessible places, like drop-down menus. Users might not know contextual menus are available, especially if your application does not use this kind of menu consistently throughout the application.

☕ Display keyboard shortcuts and mnemonics in contextual menus that are consistent with their usage in corresponding drop-down menus.

▤▷ Contextual menus are created using the `JPopupMenu` component.

Toolbars

A toolbar provides quick and convenient access to a set of frequently used commands or options. Toolbars typically contain buttons, but other components (such as text fields and combo boxes) can be placed in the toolbar as well. An optional, textured "drag area" on the toolbar indicates that users can drag the toolbar anywhere in the window or into a separate window. The drag area is on the leading edge when the toolbar is horizontal and on the top when it is vertical.

The following figure shows a toolbar with a drag area on the leading edge. For another example, see Figure 8 on page 8.

FIGURE 104 Horizontal Toolbar

Drag area ——————→

Users typically access the components in the toolbar by clicking. For information on the keyboard operations that are appropriate for toolbars, see Table 31 on page 203.

☕ Include commonly used menu items as buttons or components in your toolbar.

☕ Make special provisions for toolbar accessibility if your window does not have menus. Such provisions might include a text identifier, either as button text or in text below the button. Be sure to provide a mnemonic for such text.

Toolbar Placement   In general, a toolbar is located at the edge of the window or area on which it operates.

☕ If your window has a menu bar, place the toolbar horizontally immediately under the menu bar.

☕ Limit your window to a single toolbar with a single row of buttons or components. Multiple toolbar rows create clutter and make the features harder to find.

Draggable Toolbars   You can specify that your toolbar be draggable. Users can then move it or display it in a separate window. Users drag the toolbar by holding the mouse button down over the drag area. An outline of the toolbar moves as the user moves the pointer. The outline provides an indication of where the toolbar will appear when the user releases the mouse button. When the pointer is over a "hot spot," the outline has a dark border, indicating the toolbar will anchor to an edge of the container, as shown in the following figure. The toolbar automatically changes its orientation between horizontal and vertical depending on the edge of the window where it anchors.

FIGURE 105 Outline of a Toolbar Being Dragged

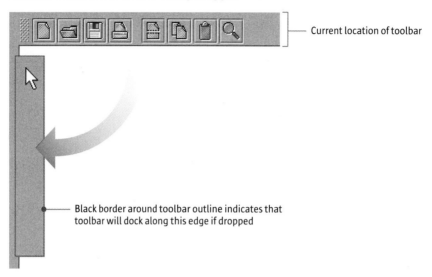

— Current location of toolbar

— Black border around toolbar outline indicates that
toolbar will dock along this edge if dropped

If the pointer is outside a hot spot, the outline has a light border, indicating that the toolbar will be displayed in a separate window. The following figure shows the toolbar in a separate window. When the user closes the window, the toolbar returns to its original location.

FIGURE 106 Toolbar in a Separate Window

A toolbar can dock (attach) along the top, bottom, left, or right edge of a container.

Toolbar Buttons   A **toolbar button** is a command button or toggle button that appears in a toolbar, typically as part of a set of such buttons. Toolbar buttons can also act as titles to display menus. In other contexts, command buttons typically use text to specify the operation or state they represent, but toolbar buttons typically use graphics.

Toolbar graphics can be difficult for users to understand. Weigh the comprehensibility of your graphics against the space taken up by button text before deciding whether to use button text in addition to the button graphics.

☕ Use button graphics that are either 16 x 16 or 24 x 24 pixels (but not both in the same toolbar), depending on the space available in your application.

☕ If you use text on the toolbar buttons, provide a user setting to display only the graphics. Using this mode, you can conserve space and display more commands and settings in the toolbar.

☕ To facilitate keyboard access, define a mnemonic for each toolbar button (or other component) that has text.

Toolbar Button Spacing and Padding   This section contains the vertical (padding) and horizontal (spacing) measurements for toolbar buttons in toolbars. The following figure shows the padding and spacing between individual toolbar buttons and groups of toolbar buttons.

☕ Space individual toolbar buttons 2 pixels apart. Space groups of toolbar buttons 11 pixels apart.

☕ Include 3 pixels of padding above and below toolbar buttons. This actually means 2 pixels of padding below the toolbar because of the white border on the buttons.

FIGURE 107 Toolbar Button Spacing

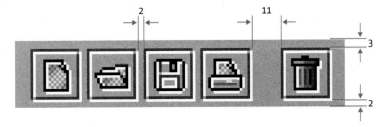

🖌 The inset on toolbar buttons should be 0.

Mouse-over Borders   To conserve space, you can use mouse-over borders (also called "rollover borders") on toolbar buttons. This border appears around a button when users move the pointer over it; otherwise, the border is invisible.

The following figure shows a toolbar button with a mouse-over border activated for the Open button.

FIGURE 108 Mouse-over Border on a Toolbar Button

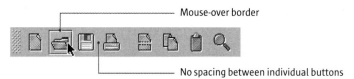

☕ When you use mouse-over borders, space individual toolbar buttons zero pixels apart within a group.

▦⊃ The `JToolBar.isRollover` client property is set to true to enable mouse-over borders.

Drop-down Menus in Toolbar Buttons   You can attach a drop-down menu to a toolbar button. The menu appears when the user clicks (or presses and holds the mouse button over) the toolbar button. The following figure shows a drop-down menu indicated by a **drop-down arrow** on the Open button. The menu provides a list of files to open.

FIGURE 109 Toolbar Button With a Drop-down Menu

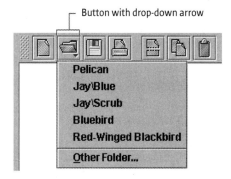

☕ Provide a drop-down arrow in the graphic for any toolbar button that has a drop-down menu.

Tool Tips for Toolbar Buttons   You can provide tool tips for the toolbar components. The tool tip displays information about the component when the user rests the pointer on it. If you specify a keyboard shortcut for a toolbar component, the JFC displays it in the tool tip. The following figure shows a tool tip that describes the Cut button.

FIGURE 110 Tool Tip for a Toolbar Button

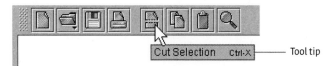

🝁 Keyboard shortcuts for toolbar buttons should match the keyboard shortcuts for the corresponding menu items.

🝁 Attach tool tips to all toolbar components that do not include text identifiers. Tool tips are valuable for all toolbar components because they display keyboard shortcuts.

🝁 If your application does not have menus, attach tool tips to the toolbar buttons in order to display keyboard shortcuts.

Tool Tips

A **tool tip** provides information about a component or area when the user rests the pointer on it (and does not press a mouse button). These small rectangles of text can be used anywhere in your application. A tool tip is commonly associated with an interface element, where it provides a short description of the component's function. If a component has a keyboard shortcut, the shortcut is automatically displayed in the tool tip.

The following figure shows a tool tip that describes a slider.

FIGURE 111 Tool Tip for a Slider

You can also use tool tips with graphics. A graphic might have one tool tip that provides the name and size of the graphic or several tool tips that describe different areas of the graphic.

The following figure shows a tool tip on an area of the bar chart in the sample applet, Retirement Savings Calculator.

FIGURE 112 Tool Tip on an Area Within a Graphic

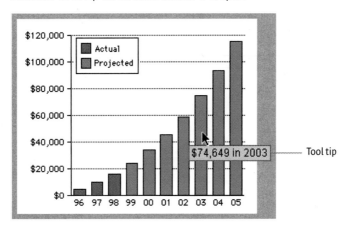

You can adjust the timing of the tool tips in your application. By default, a tool tip appears after the user rests the pointer on the component or area for 750 milliseconds. It disappears after four seconds or when the user activates the component or moves the pointer off the component.

For keyboard operations in tool tips, see Table 30 on page 203.

Make tool tips active by default, but provide users a way to turn them off. For example, you might provide a checkbox in either a menu or in a preferences dialog box.

A tool tip is specified in its associated component (and not by calling the `JToolTip` class directly).

All components need to have an `AccessibleName` set. However, interactive components that provide a descriptive tool tip don't need to have an `AccessibleDescription` set.

For details on the Java 2 Accessibility API, see "Support for Accessibility" on page 16.

10: BASIC CONTROLS

Buttons, combo boxes, and sliders are examples of controls—interface elements users can manipulate to perform an action, select an option, or set a value. A **button** is a control that users click to perform an action, set or toggle a state, or set an option. In the Java look and feel, buttons include command and toggle buttons, toolbar buttons, checkboxes, and radio buttons. A **combo box** is a control that enables users to select one option from an associated list; users can also type a choice into an editable combo box. A **slider** is a control that enables users to set a value in a range.

A **progress bar** is an interface element that indicates one or more operations are in progress and shows users what proportion of the operation has been completed. In contrast to the other components in this chapter, no user manipulation is involved.

FIGURE 113 Buttons, Combo Box, Slider, and Progress Bar

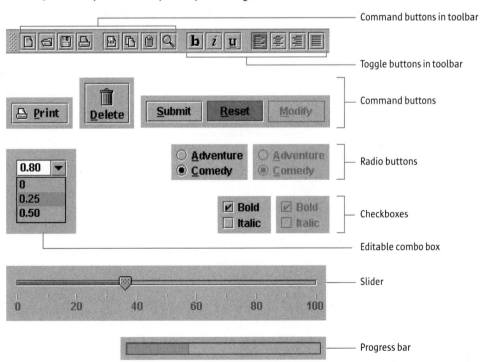

— Command buttons in toolbar

— Toggle buttons in toolbar

— Command buttons

— Radio buttons

— Checkboxes

— Editable combo box

— Slider

— Progress bar

☕ For text in buttons, sliders, and combo boxes, use headline capitalization.

🌐 Make sure you use the appropriate layout manager to lay out your controls so they allow for the longer text strings frequently associated with localization.

Command Buttons

A **command button** is a button with a rectangular border that contains text, a graphic, or both. These buttons typically use button text, often a single word, to identify the action or setting that the button represents. See "Command Buttons in Dialog Boxes" on page 115 for a list of commonly used command button names and their recommended usage.

Command buttons can stand alone or appear in a row, as shown in the following illustration.

FIGURE 114 Command Buttons

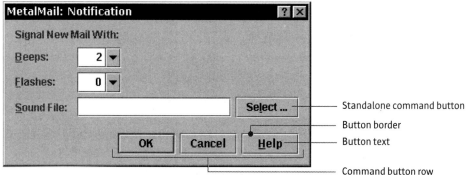

Command buttons that appear in toolbars are called "toolbar buttons." The following figure shows toolbar buttons for a text-editing application. See "Toolbar Buttons" on page 142 for details.

FIGURE 115 Toolbar Buttons

When a command button is unavailable, the dimmed appearance indicates that it cannot be used. The following figure shows the appearance of available, pressed, and dimmed command buttons.

FIGURE 116 Available, Pressed, and Unavailable Command Buttons

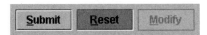

Users can click command buttons to specify a command or initiate an action, such as Save, Cancel, or Submit Changes.

For a list of keyboard operations for the activation of command buttons, see Table 15 on page 193.

 Display mnemonics in button text, with the exception of default command buttons and the Cancel button in dialog boxes. To make command buttons without text more accessible, set tool tips that describe or name the functions of the buttons.

For general details on keyboard operations and mnemonics, see "Keyboard Operations" on page 82 and "Mnemonics" on page 88. For details on displaying a command button's tool tip, see Table 30 on page 203.

For details on layout and spacing of command buttons, see "Command Button Spacing" on page 151.

Default Command Buttons   One of the buttons in any window can be the **default command button**. The JFC gives default command buttons a heavier border.

Default command buttons typically appear in dialog boxes. The default command button is activated when users press Return or Enter. A default command button (such as Save in the following figure) should represent the action most often performed, assuming that the action will not lead to loss of user data.

FIGURE 117 Default and Nondefault Command Buttons

The Enter and Return equivalents work unless keyboard focus is currently on a component that accepts the Enter or Return key. For instance, if the insertion point is in a multiline text area and the user presses Return, the insertion point moves to the beginning of a new line rather than activating a default button. Keyboard focus must be moved to another component before the default button can be activated with the keyboard.

The JFC does not automatically implement the Escape key as the keyboard equivalent for the Cancel button, so you must implement this behavior. As with the Enter and Return keys for the default command button, the Cancel button should not require keyboard focus to be activated by the Escape key.

Since you are not required to have a default button in every circumstance, you can use discretion about including them in your interface elements.

☕ Never make an unsafe choice the default button. For instance, a button that would result in discarding unsaved changes should not be the default command button.

☕ Do not supply mnemonics for the default and Cancel buttons.

Combining Graphics With Text in Command Buttons

In some circumstances, you might use a graphic along with text to identify the action or setting represented by a command button.

FIGURE 118 Command Buttons Containing Both Text and Graphics

☕ Place the text after or below the image in command buttons containing both text and graphics.

☕ Include mnemonics in your command button text—with the exception of the default and Cancel buttons.

For a list of commonly used mnemonics, see Table 10 on page 90.

Using Ellipses in Command Buttons

In circumstances in which a command button does not fully specify an action or operation and a dialog box finishes the specification, you can notify the user that this situation is about to occur by placing an ellipsis mark after the button text. For example, after clicking a Print... button, users are presented with a dialog box in which to specify printer location, how many copies to print, and so forth. By contrast, a Print command that prints one copy to the default printer without displaying a dialog box would not require an ellipsis mark.

☕ When users must view a dialog box to finish the specification of a command initiated in a command button, use an ellipsis mark (...) after the button text. When a full specification of the command is made in the button text, do not use ellipses.

Command Button Spacing For a consistent appearance, follow the guidelines described in this section to create padding within and space between command buttons. The following figure shows button text (Help) centered in a command button.

☕ Center the button text within buttons.

FIGURE 119 Command Button Text With Centered Text

🌐 Since the length and height of translated text varies, use layout managers properly to allow for differences.

Command Button Padding The blank space between the button text and the button border is referred to as "command button padding." Often command buttons appear in groups within a dialog box or an applet. In such a case, the button in the group with the widest text determines the inner padding, as shown in the following figure. Here the Cancel button has the widest text. The padding is 12 pixels on either side of the button text. The other buttons in the group (OK and Help) have the same width as the Cancel button.

☕ Determine which button has the widest button text, and insert 12 pixels of padding on either side of the text. Make all the remaining buttons in the group the same size as the button with the longest text.

☕ Space buttons in a group 5 pixels apart. (Because of the white border on the right side of a button, the apparent spacing will be 6 pixels.)

FIGURE 120 Spacing in Command Button Groups

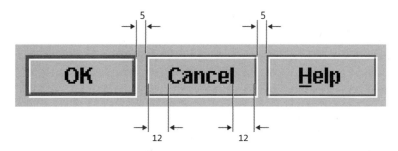

Toggle Buttons

A **toggle button** is a button that represents a setting with two states—on and off. Toggle buttons look similar to command buttons and display a graphic or text that identifies the button. The graphic or button text should remain the same whether the button is in the on or off state.

Users can click toggle buttons to turn a setting on or off—for instance, to toggle between italic and plain style in selected text.

You can use toggle buttons to represent an independent choice, like checkboxes (see page 154), or an exclusive choice within a set, like radio buttons (see page 155).

Toggle buttons can be placed in a button group to get radio button behavior.

Independent Choice

An independent toggle button behaves like a checkbox. Whether it appears alone or with other buttons, its setting is independent of other controls. An example of an independent toggle button is a Bold button on a toolbar, as shown in the following illustration.

FIGURE 121 Independent Toggle Buttons in a Toolbar

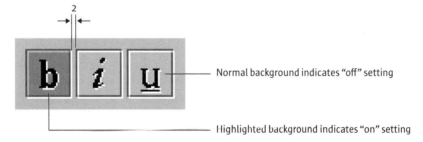

When users click the Bold button, it is highlighted to indicate that the bold style has been applied to the selection or that text to be entered will be bold. If the button is clicked again, it reverts to the normal button appearance and the bold style is removed from the selection.

Although checkboxes and independent toggle buttons have the same function, as a general rule, use checkboxes in dialog boxes and toggle buttons with a graphic in toolbars.

When toggle buttons are independent (like checkboxes) and used outside a toolbar, separate them with 5 pixels. Within a toolbar, separate independent toggle buttons by 2 pixels.

For details on the spacing of toggle buttons, see "Command Button Spacing" on page 151.

Exclusive Choice   A toggle button can also work as part of a group to represent an exclusive choice within the set. A common example is a set of toolbar toggle buttons representing left, centered, and right text alignment along with justification, as shown in the following figure.

FIGURE 122 Standard Separation of Exclusive Toggle Buttons

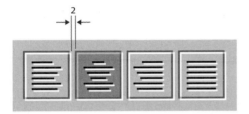

If users click the button representing left alignment, the button is highlighted to indicate that text is aligned flush with the left border of the document. If users then click the button representing centered alignment, the appearance of the Align Left button reverts to the normal button appearance and the Center button is highlighted to indicate centered alignment of the selected text.

You can use grouped toggle buttons with labels equally well in toolbars or dialog boxes. In the following example, the label identifies the abbreviations in the button text in a dialog box.

FIGURE 123 Grouped Toggle Buttons With a Label

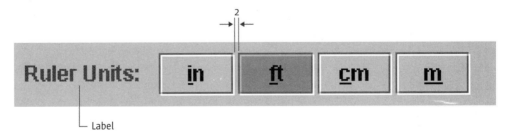

When toggle buttons form a radio set, separate them with 2 pixels.

Checkboxes

A **checkbox** is a control that represents a setting or value with an on or off choice. The setting of an individual checkbox is independent of other checkboxes—that is, more than one checkbox in a set can be checked at any given time.

A check mark within the checkbox indicates that the setting is selected. The following figure shows both active and inactive checkboxes in selected and nonselected states.

FIGURE 124 Checkboxes

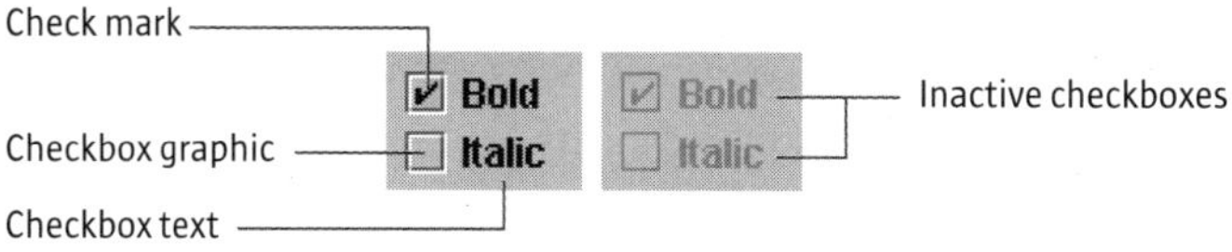

When the user clicks a checkbox, its setting toggles between off and on. When a checkbox is disabled, the user cannot change its setting.

For a list of keyboard operations for checkboxes, see Table 13 on page 192.

Use the checkbox graphic that is supplied with the component (the square box with the check mark inside).

Display checkbox text to the right of the graphic unless the application is designed for locales with right-to-left writing systems, such as Arabic and Hebrew. In this case, display the text to the left of the graphic.

Although checkboxes and independent toggle buttons have the same function, use checkboxes in dialog boxes and use toggle buttons with a graphic in toolbars.

The `setMnemonic` method can be used to specify mnemonics in checkboxes.

In addition to standard checkboxes, the JFC includes a component that is the functional equivalent of the checkbox for use in menus. See "Checkbox Menu Items" on page 135 for more information.

Checkbox Spacing

This section provides the spacing guidelines for checkbox components. As shown in the following figure, the height of the checkbox square doesn't change in an inactive checkbox even though the white highlight border is not drawn. Hence, while the checkbox is the same size, the last row and column of pixels on the bottom and right are the same color as the background canvas. The apparent spacing is 6 pixels between components; however, the actual spacing is 5 pixels.

FIGURE 125 Checkbox Spacing

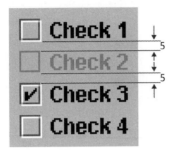

☕ Space checkboxes 5 pixels apart.

▱⊃ Use the appropriate layout manager to achieve consistent spacing in checkbox button groups.

Radio Buttons

A **radio button** represents an exclusive choice within a set of related options. Within a set of radio buttons, only one button can be on at any given time. The following figure shows active radio buttons and inactive radio buttons in both on and off states.

FIGURE 126 Radio Buttons

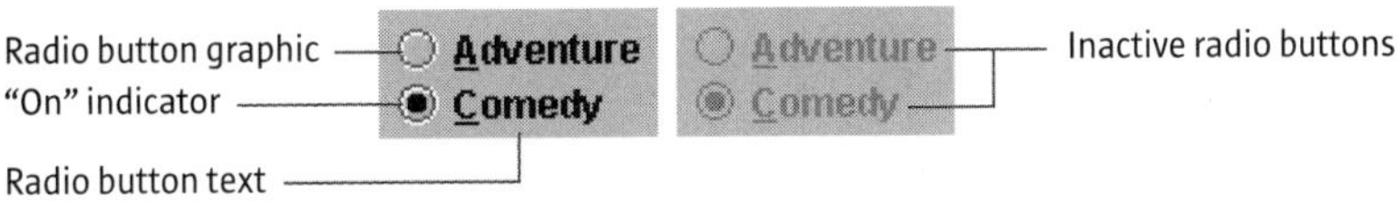

Radio button graphic ——— ○ **Adventure**   ○ Adventure ——— Inactive radio buttons
"On" indicator ——— ● **Comedy**   ● Comedy ———

Radio button text ———

When users click a radio button, its setting is always set to on. An inner filled circle within the round button indicates that the setting is selected. If another button in the set has previously been selected, its state changes to off. When a radio button is inactive, users cannot change its setting.

For a list of keyboard operations for radio buttons, see Table 21 on page 196.

☕ Use the supplied radio button graphics (the open buttons with inner filled circles).

🌐 Display radio button text to the right of the graphic unless the application is designed for locales with right-to-left writing systems, such as Arabic and Hebrew. In those locales, place the text to the left of the graphic.

☕ Although radio buttons and toggle buttons in a radio set have the same function, use radio buttons in dialog boxes and use grouped toggle buttons with graphics in toolbars. Grouped toggle buttons with text identifiers work well in either situation.

The JFC includes a component that is the functional equivalent of the radio button for use in menus. See "Radio Button Menu Items" on page 135 for more information.

Radio Button Spacing

This section provides guidelines for the spacing of radio buttons. The height of the radio button is 12 pixels, not counting the white highlight border. Inactive radio buttons do not have white borders. Hence, while the radio button is the same size, the last row and column of pixels on the bottom and right are the same color as the background canvas. As shown in the following figure, the apparent spacing is 6 pixels between components; however, the actual spacing is 5 pixels.

FIGURE 127 Radio Button Spacing

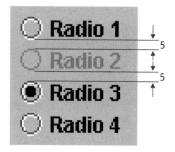

☕ Space radio buttons 5 pixels apart, as shown in the preceding figure.

▤▭ Use the appropriate layout manager to achieve consistent spacing in radio button groups.

Combo Boxes

A combo box is a component with a drop-down arrow that users click to display an associated list of choices. If the list is too long to display fully, a vertical scrollbar appears.

The currently selected item appears in the combo box. As users move the pointer over the list, each option under the pointer is highlighted. An option chosen from the list will replace the current selection. In the following figure, the currently selected option is Vanilla, and the Guanabana option will replace Vanilla when the combo box is closed.

FIGURE 128 Combo Box Display

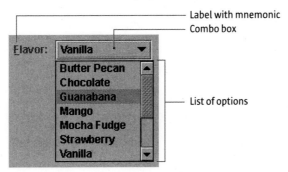

Users can close either editable or noneditable combo boxes by clicking the drop-down arrow in the combo box again, choosing an item from the list, or clicking anywhere outside the combo box.

For a list of keyboard operations appropriate for combo boxes, see Table 14 on page 192.

You can use combo boxes to provide a way for users to indicate a choice from a set of mutually exclusive options. Noneditable combo boxes enable users to choose one item from a limited set of items. Editable combo boxes provide users the additional option of typing in an item.

Use headline capitalization for the text in the items in the combo box list.

To facilitate keyboard access, provide labels with mnemonics for combo boxes.

In the JFC, the term "combo box" includes both of what Microsoft Windows applications call "list boxes" and "combo boxes."

Noneditable Combo Boxes   Noneditable combo boxes (sometimes called "list boxes" or "pop-up menus") display a list from which users can select one item.

The following figure shows a noneditable combo box with a drop-down arrow to the right of the currently selected item. (Note the gray background in the default Java look and feel theme, indicating that users cannot edit text.)

FIGURE 129 Noneditable Combo Box

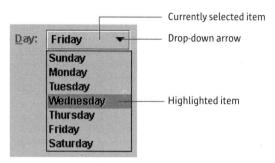

To make a selection, users have two options:

- They can click the combo box to display the list, position the pointer over the desired option to highlight it, and click.

- They can drag through the combo box to the desired choice and release the mouse button.

In either case, the currently selected item changes to reflects the choice.

You can use a noneditable combo box instead of a group of radio buttons or a list if space is limited in your application.

Editable Combo Boxes   Editable combo boxes combine a text field with a drop-down arrow that users click to display an associated list of options. As shown in the following figure, editable combo boxes initially appear as editable text fields with a drop-down arrow. The white background of the editable combo box indicates that users can type, select, and edit text.

FIGURE 130 Editable Combo Box

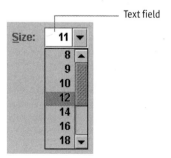

To make a choice, users have three options:

- They can click the drop-down arrow to display the list, position the pointer over the desired option to highlight it, and click.

- They can drag from the drop-down arrow to the desired choice and release the mouse button.

- To make a customized choice, they can type text in the field and press Enter or Return or move focus to another component. If the list is open, it will close.

You can use an editable combo box to save users time by making the most likely menu choices available while still enabling users to type other values in the text field. An example might be the specification of a font size. The combo box might initially display the current size, say 12. Users could select from a list of standard sizes (10, 12, 14, 18, or 24 points) or type in their own values—for instance, 22 points.

☕ Whenever possible, interpret user input into an editable combo box in a case-insensitive way. For example, it should not matter whether the user types Blue, blue, or BLUE.

▦▭ You can specify the maximum number of items to be displayed before a scrollbar appears.

Sliders

A slider is a control that is used to select a value from a continuous or discontinuous range. The position of the indicator reflects the current value. Major tick marks indicate large divisions along the range of values (for instance, every ten units); minor tick marks indicate smaller divisions (for instance, every five units).

The default slider in the Java look and feel is a nonfilling slider. An example is a slider that adjusts left-right balance in a stereo speaker system, as shown in the following figure.

FIGURE 131 Nonfilling Slider

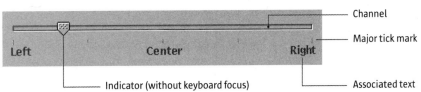

A filling slider is also available. The filled portion of the channel, shown in the following figure, represents the range of values below the current value.

FIGURE 132 Filling Slider

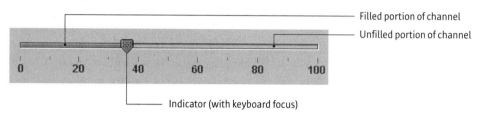

Users can drag the indicator to set a specific value or click the channel to move back and forth by one unit. Sliders can represent a series of discrete values, in which case the indicator snaps to the value closest to the end point of the drag operation.

For a list of keyboard operations for sliders, see Table 23 on page 197.

You can:

- Indicate values along the slider with major and minor tick marks, which can also have associated text

- Choose a filling or nonfilling slider

☕ If the slider represents a continuous range or a large number of discrete values and the exact value that is chosen is important, provide a text field where the chosen value can be displayed. For instance, a user might want to specify an annual retirement savings contribution of 2.35%. In such a situation, consider making the text field editable to give users the option of typing in the value directly.

▱ The JSlider.isFilled client property can be used to enable the optional filling slider.

Progress Bars
A progress bar indicates that one or more operations is under way and shows users what proportion of the operation has been completed. The progress bar consists of a rectangular bar that fills as the operation progresses, as shown in the following figure.

FIGURE 133 Progress Bar

Users cannot interact with a progress bar. If you would like to enable users to set a value in a range, use the slider component, described on page 159.

You can orient the progress bar horizontally, so it fills from left to right, or vertically, so it fills from bottom to top. Within the bounds of the progress bar, you can display a text message that is updated as the bar fills. By default, the message shows the percentage of the process completed—for example, 25%.

The following figure shows another use of the progress bar. In this example of a process control application, the progress bar is not used to track the progress of an operation; rather, it is used as a gauge to show the temperature of a vat in a candy factory. The temperature indicates the proportion of the maximum temperature that has been reached (more than three-quarters), and the text message within the progress bar specifies the exact value (114 degrees).

FIGURE 134 Text Inside a Progress Bar

☕ If you create your own message to display inside the progress bar, make it concise.

11: TEXT COMPONENTS

Text components enable users to view and edit text in an application. The simplest text component you can provide is a **label,** which presents read-only information. A label is usually associated with another component and describes its function. A **text field** is a rectangular area that displays a single line of text, which can be editable or noneditable. A **password field** is an editable text field that displays masking characters in place of the characters that the user types.

Other text components display multiple lines of text. A **text area** displays text in a single font, size, and style. You can configure an **editor pane** to display different types of text through the use of a plug-in editor. These editors include a plain text editor, a styled text editor, an RTF (rich text format) editor, and an HTML (Hypertext Markup Language) editor.

FIGURE 135 Text Components

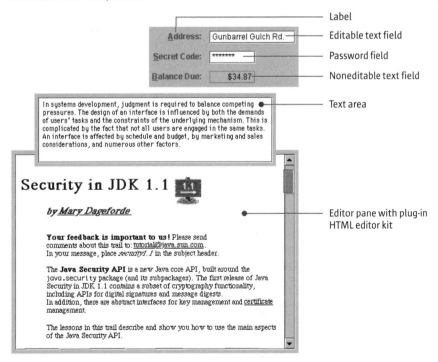

⊕ Make your text easier to localize by using resource bundles. A resource bundle stores text separately so that localizers don't have to change the application's source code to accommodate translation.

For guidelines on translating text, see "Planning for Internationalization and Localization" on page 33.

Labels

A label consists of read-only text, graphics, or both. Labels serve two functions in an application: to identify components and to communicate status and other information. Users cannot select a label.

Labels That Identify Controls

You can associate a label with a component (such as a text field, slider, or checkbox) to describe the use of the component. In the following figure, the Salary Contribution: label lets users know they can use the slider to adjust their salary contribution.

FIGURE 136 Label That Describes the Use of a Slider

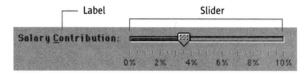

You can also use a label to describe a group of components. In the following figure, the Color: label describes a group of three radio buttons. The text (Red, Yellow, and Blue) is part of the radio buttons and not a separate component, as is the Color: label.

FIGURE 137 Label That Describes a Radio Button Group

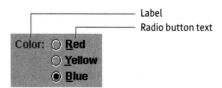

☕ Keep the text of the label brief, and use terminology that is familiar to users.

Active and Inactive Labels   You can make a label active or inactive so that its state is the same as the component it describes. Active labels are drawn in the primary 1 color defined in the application's color theme. Inactive labels are drawn in the secondary 2 color defined in the application's color theme. The following figure shows an active and inactive label.

FIGURE 138 Active and Inactive Labels

 Make a label inactive when the component it describes is inactive.

Spacing, Position, and Capitalization of Labels   The following figure shows the recommended spacing, position, and capitalization of labels.

FIGURE 139 Spacing Between a Label and a Component

 Insert 12 pixels between a label and the component it describes when labels are right aligned. When labels are left aligned, insert 12 pixels between the longest label and its associated component.

 Display a label before or above the component it describes. For languages that read from left to right, "before" is to the left of the component.

 Use headline capitalization in the label text and place a colon at the end of the text.

For more information on aligning labels in the user interface, see "Text Layout" on page 52. For more information on capitalization, see "Capitalization of Text in the Interface" on page 46.

Mnemonics in Labels   You can specify a mnemonic for a label. When the mnemonic is activated, it gives focus to the component that the label describes. This technique is often used with a label that accompanies an editable text field. In the following figure, the text field gets focus when users press Alt-N.

FIGURE 140   Label With a Mnemonic

Mnemonic

☕ If you can't add a mnemonic directly to the component that requires one, as in the case of an editable text field, place the mnemonic in the component's label.

🖳▭ The displayedMnemonic property can be used to specify the mnemonic in a label.

🖳▭ The labelFor property can be used to associate a label with another component so that the component gains focus when the label's mnemonic is activated.

Labels That Communicate Status and Other Information   You can use a label to communicate status or give instructions to users. In addition, you can instruct your application to alter a label to show a change in state. The progress bar in the following figure uses two labels that change as the operation progresses. The application changes the top label to reflect the file currently being copied, and it updates the bottom label as the progress bar fills.

FIGURE 141   Labels That Clarify the Meaning of a Progress Bar

☕ Use sentence capitalization in the text of a label that communicates status.

Text Fields

A text field is a rectangular area that displays a single line of text. A text field can be editable or noneditable.

Noneditable Text Fields

In a noneditable text field, users can select and copy text, but they cannot change it. Only the application can change the contents of a noneditable text field. The background of a noneditable text field is the secondary 3 color defined in the application's color theme. In the default theme, the background color is gray, as shown in the following figure.

FIGURE 142 Noneditable Text Field

Editable Text Fields

In an editable text field, users can type or edit a single line of text. For example, a find dialog box has a text field in which users type a string for which they want to search. A text field has keyboard focus when it displays a blinking bar that indicates the insertion point. When users type in text that is too long to fit in the field, the text scrolls horizontally. By default, the background of an editable text field is white.

The following figure shows an editable text field with keyboard focus. The Language: label is a separate component from the text field.

FIGURE 143 Editable Text Field With Blinking Bar

In an editable text field, users can:

- Set the insertion point by single-clicking

- Select a word by double-clicking

- Select the entire line of text by triple-clicking

- Select a range of characters by dragging

- Insert characters and replace selected text by typing at the insertion point

- Cut, copy, and paste text by using menu commands or keyboard shortcuts (Ctrl-X for cut, Ctrl-C for copy, and Ctrl-V for paste)

The following figure shows a text field with the letters `Jeffer` selected. The insertion point is at the end of the selected text and indicates that the text field has keyboard focus. The selected text is overwritten when the user types or pastes new text.

FIGURE 144 Editable Text Field With Selected Text

Thomas Jefferson

To associate a mnemonic with a text field, you must give the text field a label. You can then assign a mnemonic to the label, and make the mnemonic give focus to the text field. For details, see "Mnemonics in Labels" on page 166. For keyboard operations appropriate to text fields, see Table 28 on page 202.

Depending on the type of data, you might be able to check individual characters for errors as they are typed—for example, if users try to type a letter into a text field that should contain only numbers. In this case, do not display the character in the field. Instead, sound the system beep. If the user types three illegal characters in a row, post an Error alert box that explains the legal entries for the text field.

If you plan an action based on the string in the text field (such as searching for the string or performing a calculation) do so when users signify that they have completed the entry by typing Enter or Return or by moving keyboard focus outside the text field.

Password Fields

The password field is an editable text field that displays a masking character instead of the characters that users type. Asterisks are displayed in the password field by default. You can designate any Unicode character as the masking character (but make sure the character is available in the current font).

The password field is commonly used in a login dialog box, as shown in the following figure. The Password: label is a separate component from the password field.

FIGURE 145 Password Field

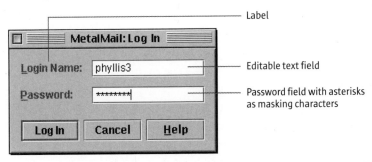

A password field provides users some of the same editing capabilities as an editable text field, but not the cut and copy operations. For keyboard operations appropriate to password fields, see Table 28 on page 202.

The `setEchoChar` method can be used to change the masking character—for example, from asterisks to pound signs.

Text Areas
A text area provides a rectangular space in which users can view, type, and edit multiple lines of text. The JFC renders such text in a single font, size, and style, as shown in the following figure.

FIGURE 146 Text Area

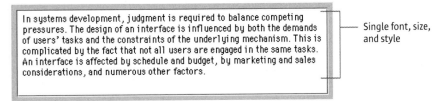

Users can type and replace text in a text area. See "Text Fields" on page 167 for a description of text-editing features supplied by the JFC. For keyboard operations appropriate to text areas, see Table 27 on page 200.

You can enable word wrap so that the text wraps to the next line when it reaches the edge of the text area, as shown in the preceding figure. You can enable scrolling by placing the text area inside a scroll pane. In this case, the text scrolls horizontally and vertically when it is too long to fit in the text area.

The following figure shows a text area inside a scroll pane. For information on scrolling, see "Scroll Panes" on page 102.

FIGURE 147 Text Area in a Scroll Pane

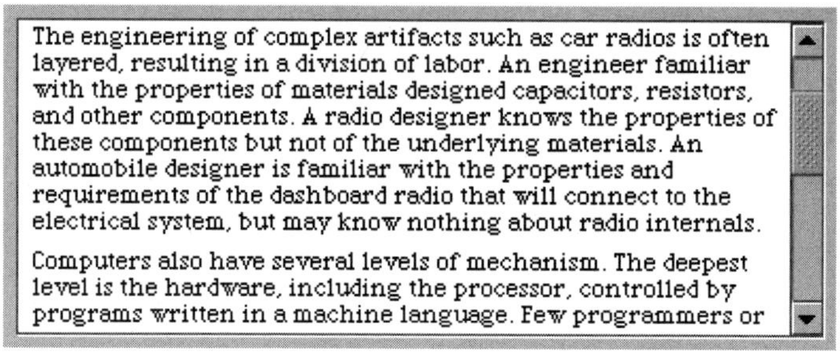

The engineering of complex artifacts such as car radios is often layered, resulting in a division of labor. An engineer familiar with the properties of materials designed capacitors, resistors, and other components. A radio designer knows the properties of these components but not of the underlying materials. An automobile designer is familiar with the properties and requirements of the dashboard radio that will connect to the electrical system, but may know nothing about radio internals.

Computers also have several levels of mechanism. The deepest level is the hardware, including the processor, controlled by programs written in a machine language. Few programmers or

The `lineWrap` and `wrapStyleWord` properties of the text area can be set to true to enable word wrap on word boundaries.

Editor Panes

An editor pane is a multiline text pane that uses a **plug-in editor kit** to display a specific type of text, such as RTF (rich text format) or HTML (Hypertext Markup Language). An editor kit is capable of displaying all fonts provided in the AWT. The JFC provides four kits that you can plug into an editor pane:

- Default editor kit
- Styled text editor kit
- RTF editor kit
- HTML editor kit

You can also create your own editor kit or use a third-party editor kit. For an example of how to create an editor kit, see *Java Swing* by Robert Eckstein, Marc Loy, and Dave Wood.

The `setEditable` method can be used to turn text editing on or off in an editor kit.

Default Editor Kit

You can use the default editor kit to display text in a single font, size, and style. This kit is functionally equivalent to a text area.

Styled Text Editor Kit

You can use a styled text editor kit to display multiple fonts, sizes, and styles, as shown in the following figure. You can also embed images and components (such as tables) in a styled text editor kit.

FIGURE 148 Styled Text Editor Kit

Figure 1. Two designs for kitchen faucets. The user interface for the faucet on the left is based on an engineering model—the faucet handles directly control the hot and cold water flows. The interface for the faucet on the right is based on a user task model—moving the handle up and down controls the combined flow rate; moving it from side to side controls the temperature.

DIFFERENT MODELS FOR AN INTERFACE

Designers of the human interface for a computer or other complex system consciously or unconsciously choose a model that will form the basis for the interface. Engineers involved in the design of the system have extensive knowledge

Multiple font sizes and styles

RTF Editor Kit You can use an RTF editor kit to read, write, and display RTF text, as shown in the following figure. The RTF editor kit also provides the capabilities provided by the styled editor kit.

FIGURE 149 RTF Editor Kit

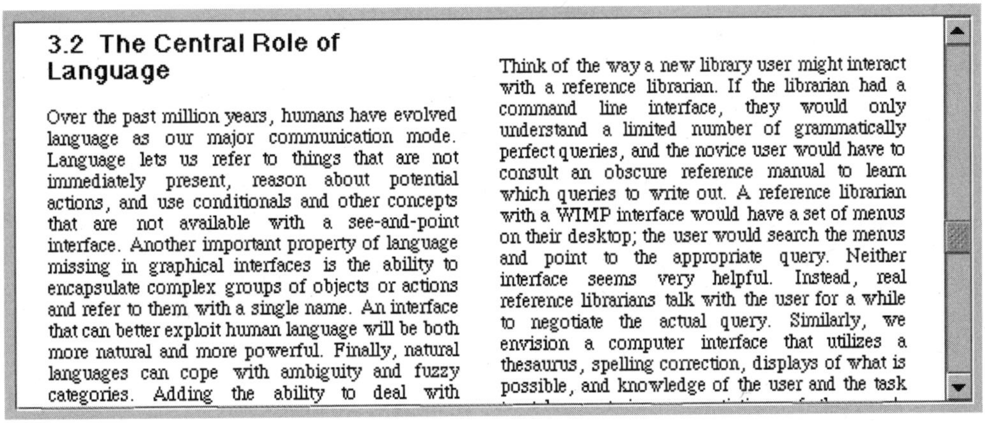

3.2 The Central Role of Language

Over the past million years, humans have evolved language as our major communication mode. Language lets us refer to things that are not immediately present, reason about potential actions, and use conditionals and other concepts that are not available with a see-and-point interface. Another important property of language missing in graphical interfaces is the ability to encapsulate complex groups of objects or actions and refer to them with a single name. An interface that can better exploit human language will be both more natural and more powerful. Finally, natural languages can cope with ambiguity and fuzzy categories. Adding the ability to deal with

Think of the way a new library user might interact with a reference librarian. If the librarian had a command line interface, they would only understand a limited number of grammatically perfect queries, and the novice user would have to consult an obscure reference manual to learn which queries to write out. A reference librarian with a WIMP interface would have a set of menus on their desktop; the user would search the menus and point to the appropriate query. Neither interface seems very helpful. Instead, real reference librarians talk with the user for a while to negotiate the actual query. Similarly, we envision a computer interface that utilizes a thesaurus, spelling correction, displays of what is possible, and knowledge of the user and the task

HTML Editor Kit   You can use an HTML editor kit to display text in HTML 3.2. Users can click a link on the HTML page to generate an event, which you can use to replace the contents in the pane.

FIGURE 150 HTML Editor Kit

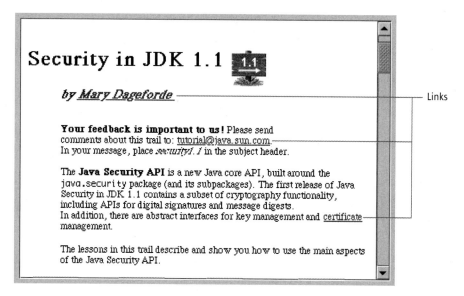

LISTS, TABLES, AND TREES

Lists, tables, and trees provide a way to organize related information so users can easily make comparisons of the data. A **list** is a one-dimensional arrangement of data, and a **table** is a two-dimensional arrangement of data. A **tree view** is an outline of hierarchical relationships.

FIGURE 151 List, Table, and Tree View

List

Bell Pepper
Mushroom
Olive
Pepperoni
Pineapple
Sausage
Smoked Ham

Table

First Name	Last Name	Employee ID	Project
Jakob	Lehn	532	Butler
Peter	Winter	27	FireDog
Sophia	Amann	377	Krakatoa
Samuel	Stewart	452	Butler
Eva	Kidney	1273	Moonbeam
Mary	Dole	811	FireDog
Roscoe	Arrowsmith	28	FireDog
Mira	Brooks	192	Moonbeam

Tree view

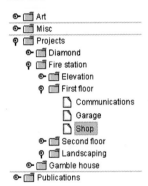

Lists

A list displays a set of items, which can be text, graphics, or both. You can use a list to present users with a set of exclusive or nonexclusive choices. For example, you might use a list to present the days of the week, from which users could choose one day on which to start their calendars. Or, you might use a list to display pizza toppings, from which users could make several selections, as shown in the following figure.

FIGURE 152 Nonexclusive List

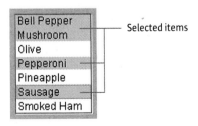

Selected items

For other components that enable users to select one item from a limited set of items, see "Noneditable Combo Boxes" on page 157 and "Radio Buttons" on page 155. For a component that enables users to select one item from a limited set of items or type in an alternative item, see "Editable Combo Boxes" on page 158. For a component that enables users to select one value from a continuous or discontinuous range of values, see "Sliders" on page 159.

For the keyboard operations appropriate for lists, see Table 19 on page 195.

☕ When resizing a list, be sure that it always displays a whole number of lines.

Scrolling

You can provide vertical and horizontal scrolling of the items in a list by placing the list inside a scroll pane. Users can then scroll the list as described in "Scroll Panes" on page 102.

☕ If you place a list in a scroll pane, make the vertical and horizontal scrollbars appear only when needed. This behavior is the default behavior of scroll panes.

Selection Models for Lists

The JFC provides three selection models that you can use to enable users to select list items: single item, single range, and multiple ranges. Single-item selection provides users with an exclusive choice. Single-range and multiple-range selection provide users with nonexclusive choices.

Single Item

You can enable users to select a single item by clicking it. The item gets keyboard focus. The prior selection, if any, is deselected. In the following figure, the user has selected Pepperoni.

FIGURE 153 Single-Item Selection in a List

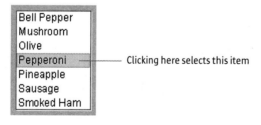

Clicking here selects this item

Single Range of Items   You can enable users to select a single item or a range of items. Users select an item by clicking it. The item gets keyboard focus and becomes the anchor point of the selection. Users extend the selection by moving the pointer to another item and Shift-clicking. In the following figure, the user first clicked Sausage and then Shift-clicked Pineapple.

FIGURE 154 Range of Selected Items in a List

Multiple Ranges of Items   You can enable users to select a single item, a range of items, or multiple ranges of items (also known as "discontinuous," "discontiguous," or "disjoint" ranges). Users select a single item by clicking it and extend the selection by Shift-clicking. To start another range, users Control-click an item. That item gets keyboard focus and becomes the anchor point of the new range. In addition, the selection of the item is toggled—if the item was initially selected, it is deselected, and vice versa. Shift-clicking extends the new range.

In the following figure, the user selected the first range by clicking Bell Pepper and then Shift-clicking Pineapple. The user selected additional ranges by Control-clicking Pepperoni and Sausage.

FIGURE 155 Multiple Ranges of Selected Items in a List

Bell Pepper	——— Clicking here selects this item and sets the anchor point
Mushroom	——— Shift-clicking here extends the selection
Olive	
Pepperoni	——— Control-clicking here selects the item and moves the anchor point
Pineapple	
Sausage	——— Control-clicking here selects the item and moves the anchor point again
Smoked Ham	

Tables

A table organizes related information into a series of rows and columns. Each field in the table is called a "cell." By default, a cell contains a text field, but you can replace it with graphics and other components, such as a checkbox or combo box. The cell with keyboard focus has an inner border, which is drawn in the primary 1 color in the application's color theme.

The following figure illustrates the use of a table to display the records of employees in a company database. The cell with the value 377 is selected and has keyboard focus.

FIGURE 156 Table in a Scroll Pane

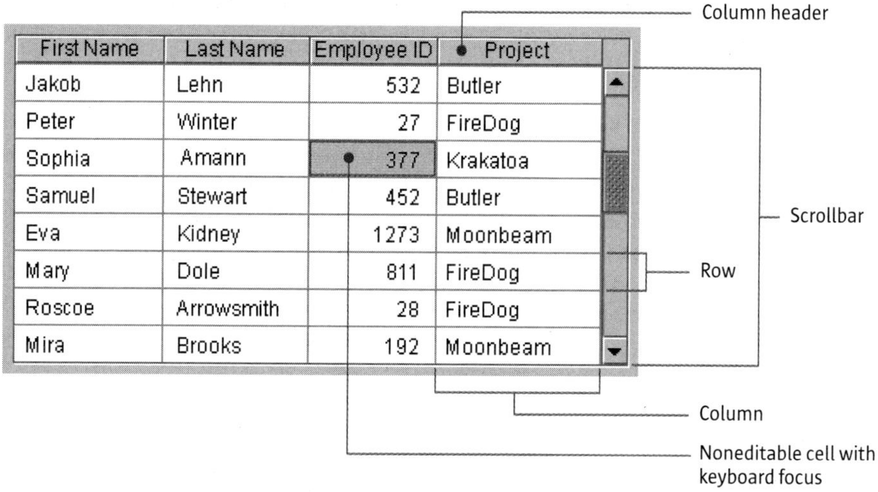

The background color of a cell depends on whether the cell is selected, whether the cell is editable, and the background color of the table. The following table shows how a cell gets its background color.

TABLE 11   Background Color of Table Cells

Type of Cell	Background Color	Example
An unselected cell (editable or noneditable)	The background color of the table, which is white by default.	Kidney
A selected cell that is editable and currently has keyboard focus	White. The inner border is drawn in the primary 1 color to indicate that the cell has keyboard focus. (For information on color themes in the Java look and feel, see "Colors" on page 40.)	Mary
Any other selected cell	The primary 3 color, which is light blue in the default color theme.	Sophia

Users can select and edit a cell if the component in that cell supports editing. For example, if a cell contains a text field, users can type, cut, copy, and paste text. For more information on editing text in a table, see "Editable Text Fields" on page 167. For the keyboard operations that are appropriate for tables, see Table 26 on page 199.

Table Appearance   The JFC provides several options that enable you to define the appearance of your table. You can turn on the display of horizontal and vertical lines that define the table cells, as shown in Figure 156 on page 176. You can set the horizontal and vertical padding around the content of a cell. You can also set the width of the columns.

When resizing a table vertically, make sure that it always displays a whole number of lines.

Table Scrolling   You can provide scrolling of your table by placing the table inside a scroll pane. A table has column headers only when it is in a scroll pane. For information on scrolling, see "Scroll Panes" on page 102.

Column Reordering   You can enable users to rearrange the columns in the table. When users drag the column header to the right or left, the entire column moves. Releasing the mouse button places the column at the new location.

The following figure shows the Last Name column being dragged to the right. In this case, the column is selected (although users can also drag an unselected column).

FIGURE 157 Reordering Columns by Dragging a Column Header

First Name	Employee ID		Last Name	oject	
Jakob	532		Lehn		
Peter	27		Winter	)g	
Sophia	377		Amann	toa	
Samuel	452		Stewart		
Eva	1273		Kidney	)ea⊓	
Mary	811		Dole	)g	
Roscoe	28		Arrowsmith	)g	
Mira	192		Brooks	)eam	

Column Resizing   You can enable users to resize the columns in a table. Users drag the right border of the column header to the right to make the column wider, and to the left to make the column narrower. When users resize a column, you must decide whether to change the width of the entire table or adjust the other columns so the overall width is preserved. The JFC-supplied resize options are described in the following table.

TABLE 12 Table Resize Options

The original table. The double arrow shows the west resize pointer before the columns are resized.	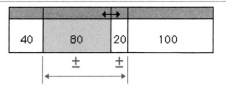 *(columns: 40, 40, 60, 100)*
Resize next Resizes the columns on either side of the border being moved. One column becomes bigger, while the other becomes smaller.	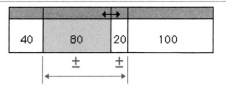 *(columns: 40, 80, 20, 100)*
Resize subsequent Resizes the column whose border was moved and all columns to its right. This option is the default option.	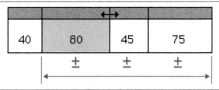 *(columns: 40, 80, 45, 75)*

TABLE 12   Table Resize Options *(Continued)*

Resize last Resizes the column whose border was moved and the last (rightmost) column.	40 80 60 60
Resize all Resizes all other columns, distributing the remaining space proportionately.	32 80 48 80
Resize off Resizes the column whose border was moved, and makes the table wider or narrower to adjust the space added or removed from the column. This is the only option that changes the overall width of the table.	40 80 60 100

Row Sorting   You can give users the ability to sort the rows in a table by clicking the column headers. An email application, which displays a list of messages in a table, is well suited for row sorting. As shown in the following figure, users can sort the messages by date, sender, or subject. The header of the From column appears in bold to indicate that the messages are currently sorted alphabetically by sender.

FIGURE 158   Row Sorting in an Email Application

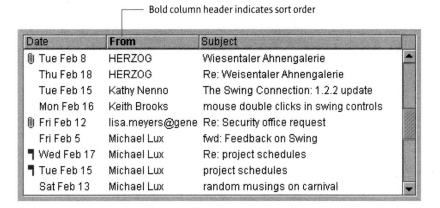

☕ Provide a visual indicator for the table column that currently determines the sort order. For example, put the column header text in bold.

☕ If your application has a menu bar, provide row sorting as a set of menu items as well (for example, include "Sort by Sender" in the View menu).

🖅 Row sorting is not included with the table component. However, the JFC contains sample code that can be used to implement row sorting. See *The Java Tutorial* for more information.

Selection Models for Tables

When designing a table, you must decide which objects (cells, rows, or columns) users can select. The JFC provides 24 models for selecting objects in tables, but they are not all distinct.

☕ The following nine selection models are recommended for use in the Java look and feel:

- No selection
- Single cell
- Single range of cells
- Single row
- Single range of rows
- Multiple ranges of rows
- Single column
- Single range of columns
- Multiple ranges of columns

No Selection   You can turn off selection in a table. Nothing is selected when users click in a cell.

Single Cell   You can enable users to select a cell by clicking it. The cell gets keyboard focus, which is indicated by an inner border. Any previous selection is deselected.

In the following figure, the cell containing 377 is selected and has keyboard focus. The cell cannot be edited, as indicated by the primary 3 background color.

FIGURE 159 Single-Cell Selection

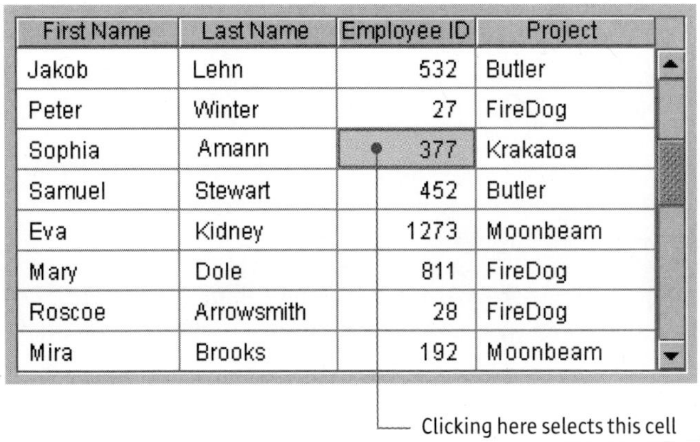

First Name	Last Name	Employee ID	Project
Jakob	Lehn	532	Butler
Peter	Winter	27	FireDog
Sophia	Amann	● 377	Krakatoa
Samuel	Stewart	452	Butler
Eva	Kidney	1273	Moonbeam
Mary	Dole	811	FireDog
Roscoe	Arrowsmith	28	FireDog
Mira	Brooks	192	Moonbeam

—— Clicking here selects this cell

Range of Cells   You can enable users to select a single cell or a rectangular range of cells. Users select a cell by clicking it. That cell gets keyboard focus and becomes the anchor point of the selection. Users extend the selection by moving the pointer to a new cell and Shift-clicking. Users can also select a range of cells by dragging through the range.

In the following figure, the user has selected the range by clicking Sophia and then Shift-clicking 1273. The cell containing Sophia is editable, as indicated by its white background.

FIGURE 160 Range of Selected Cells

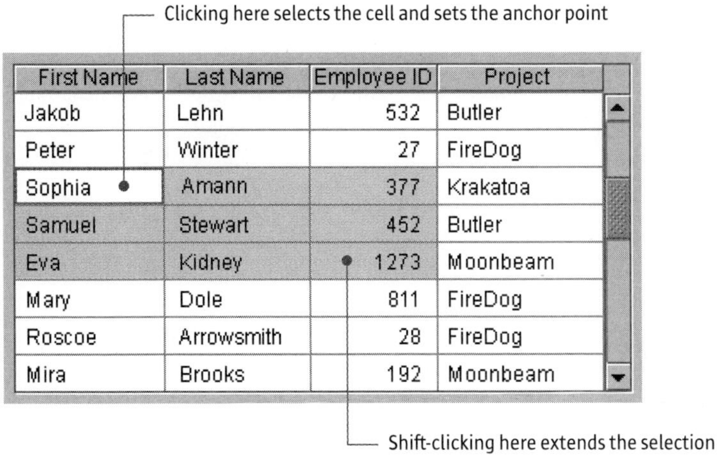

—— Clicking here selects the cell and sets the anchor point

First Name	Last Name	Employee ID	Project
Jakob	Lehn	532	Butler
Peter	Winter	27	FireDog
Sophia ●	Amann	377	Krakatoa
Samuel	Stewart	452	Butler
Eva	Kidney	● 1273	Moonbeam
Mary	Dole	811	FireDog
Roscoe	Arrowsmith	28	FireDog
Mira	Brooks	192	Moonbeam

—— Shift-clicking here extends the selection

In range selection, the selection always extends from the cell with the anchor point to the cell where the user Shift-clicked. If users move the pointer within the selection and Shift-click, the selection becomes smaller. For example, if the user Shift-clicks Stewart in the preceding figure, the selection is reduced to four cells (Sophia, Amann, Samuel, and Stewart).

Single Row   You can enable users to select an entire row by clicking any cell in the row. The clicked cell gets keyboard focus, which is indicated by an inner border. Any previous selection is deselected.

In the following figure, the user has clicked the cell containing 811. This cell is not editable, as indicated by its background color.

FIGURE 161   Single-Row Selection

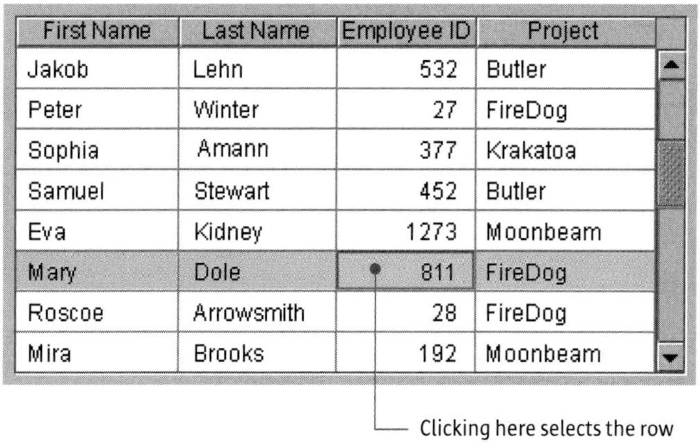

First Name	Last Name	Employee ID	Project
Jakob	Lehn	532	Butler
Peter	Winter	27	FireDog
Sophia	Amann	377	Krakatoa
Samuel	Stewart	452	Butler
Eva	Kidney	1273	Moonbeam
Mary	Dole	● 811	FireDog
Roscoe	Arrowsmith	28	FireDog
Mira	Brooks	192	Moonbeam

└── Clicking here selects the row

Single Range of Rows   You can enable users to select one row or a range of rows. Users select a row by clicking any cell in the row. The cell that has been clicked gets keyboard focus and becomes the anchor point of the selection. Users extend the selection by moving the pointer to a new row and Shift-clicking. Users can also select a range of rows by dragging through the range.

In the following figure, the user has clicked Amann and then Shift-clicked Dole. The cell containing Amann is editable, as indicated by its white background.

FIGURE 162 Range of Selected Rows

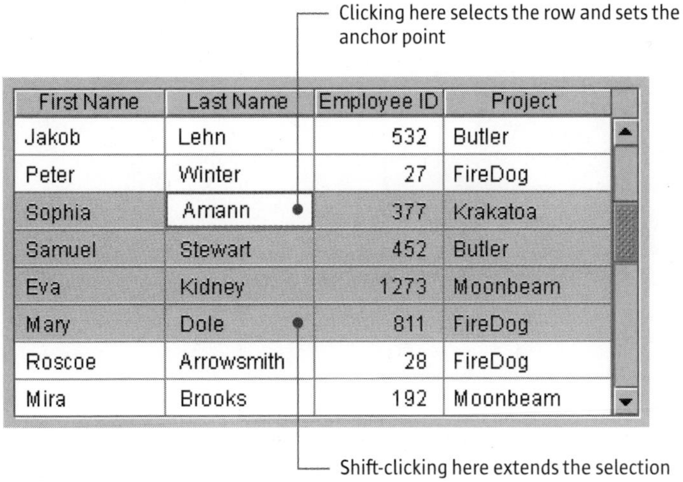

Clicking here selects the row and sets the
anchor point

First Name	Last Name	Employee ID	Project
Jakob	Lehn	532	Butler
Peter	Winter	27	FireDog
Sophia	Amann ●	377	Krakatoa
Samuel	Stewart	452	Butler
Eva	Kidney	1273	Moonbeam
Mary	Dole ●	811	FireDog
Roscoe	Arrowsmith	28	FireDog
Mira	Brooks	192	Moonbeam

Shift-clicking here extends the selection

In range selection, the selection always extends from the row with the
anchor point to the row where the user has Shift-clicked. If users Shift-click
within an existing selection, the selection becomes smaller. For example, if
the user Shift-clicks Stewart in the preceding figure, the selection is reduced
to the two rows containing Amann and Stewart.

Multiple Ranges of Rows   You can enable users to select a single row, a range of rows,
or multiple row ranges (also known as "discontinuous," "discontiguous," or
"disjoint" ranges). Users select a single row by clicking any cell in the row
and extend the selection by Shift-clicking. To start another range, users
Control-click any cell in a row. The cell gets keyboard focus and becomes the
anchor point of the new range. The selection of the row toggles as follows:

- If the row is not already selected, it is selected. A subsequent Shift-click
  selects all rows from the anchor point to the row where the user has
  Shift-clicked.

- If the row is within an existing selection, the row is deselected. A
  subsequent Shift-click deselects all rows from the anchor point to the
  row where the user has Shift-clicked.

Users can also select another range by dragging through the range while
holding down the Control key.

In the following figure, the user has selected the first range by clicking
Winter and then Shift-clicking Amann. The user has created another range by
Control-clicking Mary and then Shift-clicking Roscoe. The cell containing Mary
has keyboard focus and is editable.

FIGURE 163 Multiple Ranges of Selected Rows

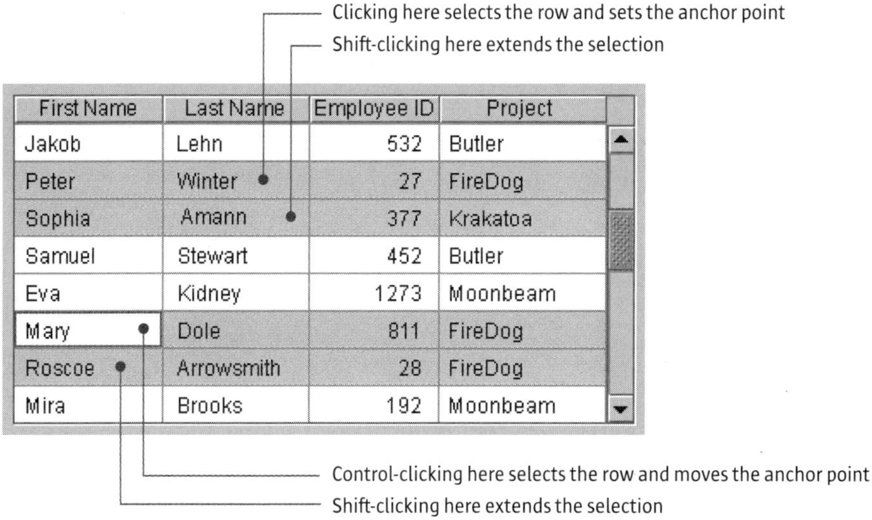

Clicking here selects the row and sets the anchor point
Shift-clicking here extends the selection

First Name	Last Name	Employee ID	Project
Jakob	Lehn	532	Butler
Peter	Winter	27	FireDog
Sophia	Amann	377	Krakatoa
Samuel	Stewart	452	Butler
Eva	Kidney	1273	Moonbeam
Mary	Dole	811	FireDog
Roscoe	Arrowsmith	28	FireDog
Mira	Brooks	192	Moonbeam

Control-clicking here selects the row and moves the anchor point
Shift-clicking here extends the selection

Multiple-range selection is well suited for an email application that uses a
table to display message headers, as shown in Figure 158 on page 179. Users
can select one or more message headers (especially useful for deleting
messages).

Single Column Only You can enable users to select an entire column by clicking any
cell in the column. The cell that was clicked gets keyboard focus, which is
indicated by an inner border. Any previous selection is deselected.

In the following figure, the user has clicked Amann in the Last Name column.
The white background indicates that the cell can be edited.

FIGURE 164 Single-Column Selection

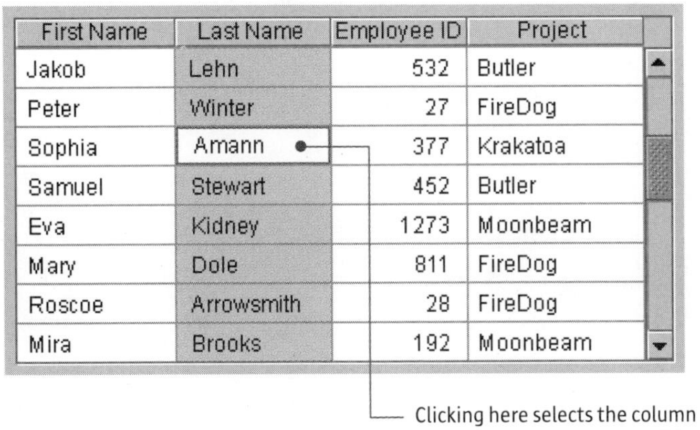

First Name	Last Name	Employee ID	Project
Jakob	Lehn	532	Butler
Peter	Winter	27	FireDog
Sophia	Amann	377	Krakatoa
Samuel	Stewart	452	Butler
Eva	Kidney	1273	Moonbeam
Mary	Dole	811	FireDog
Roscoe	Arrowsmith	28	FireDog
Mira	Brooks	192	Moonbeam

—— Clicking here selects the column

Single Range of Columns   You can enable users to select one column or a range of columns. Users select a column by clicking any cell in the column. The cell that was clicked gets keyboard focus and becomes the anchor point of the selection. Users extend the selection by moving the pointer to a new column and Shift-clicking. Users can also select a range of columns by dragging through the range.

In the following figure, the user has clicked 1273 and then Shift-clicked Amann. The cell containing 1273 cannot be edited, as indicated by its background color.

FIGURE 165 Range of Selected Columns

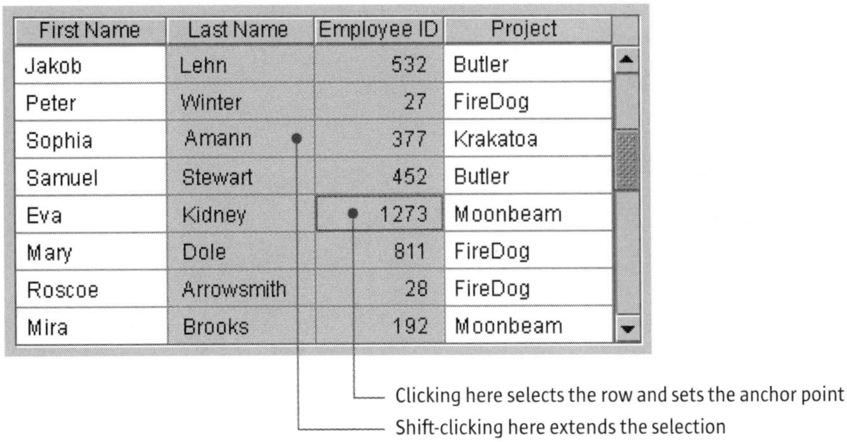

First Name	Last Name	Employee ID	Project
Jakob	Lehn	532	Butler
Peter	Winter	27	FireDog
Sophia	Amann	377	Krakatoa
Samuel	Stewart	452	Butler
Eva	Kidney	1273	Moonbeam
Mary	Dole	811	FireDog
Roscoe	Arrowsmith	28	FireDog
Mira	Brooks	192	Moonbeam

—— Clicking here selects the row and sets the anchor point
—— Shift-clicking here extends the selection

In range selection, the selection always extends from the column with the anchor point to the column where the user has Shift-clicked. If users Shift-click within an existing selection, the selection becomes smaller.

Multiple Ranges of Columns   You can enable users to select a single column, a range of columns, or multiple-column ranges (also known as "discontinuous," "discontiguous," or "disjoint" ranges). Users select a single column by clicking any cell in the column and extend the selection by Shift-clicking. To start another range, users Control-click any cell in the column. The cell gets keyboard focus and becomes the anchor point of the range. The selection of the column toggles as follows:

- If the column is not already selected, it is selected. A subsequent Shift-click selects all columns from the anchor point to the column where the user Shift-clicked.

- If the column is within an existing selection, the column is deselected. A subsequent Shift-click deselects all columns from the anchor point to the column where the user Shift-clicked.

Users can also select another range by dragging through the range while holding down the Control key.

In the following figure, the user has clicked Peter and then Shift-clicked Amann. The user has selected another range by Control-clicking Krakatoa, which has keyboard focus and can be edited, as indicated by its white background.

FIGURE 166 Multiple Ranges of Selected Columns

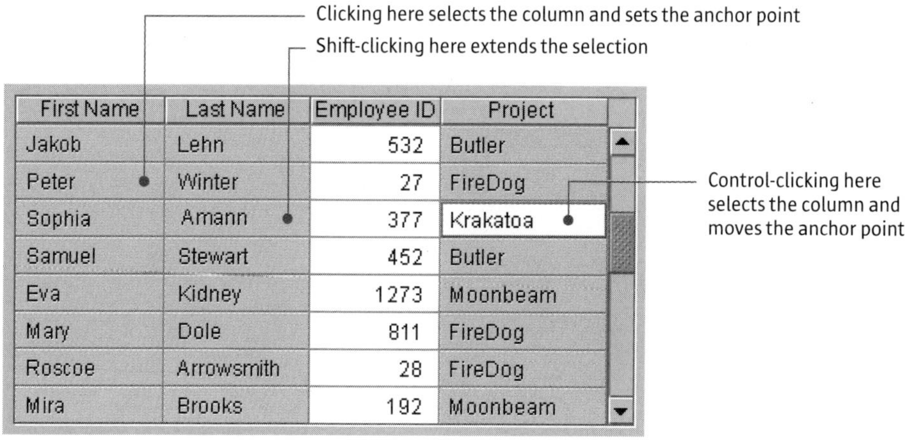

Clicking here selects the column and sets the anchor point
Shift-clicking here extends the selection

First Name	Last Name	Employee ID	Project	
Jakob	Lehn	532	Butler	▲
Peter ●	Winter	27	FireDog	
Sophia	Amann ●	377	Krakatoa ●	
Samuel	Stewart	452	Butler	
Eva	Kidney	1273	Moonbeam	
Mary	Dole	811	FireDog	
Roscoe	Arrowsmith	28	FireDog	
Mira	Brooks	192	Moonbeam	▼

Control-clicking here selects the column and moves the anchor point

Tree Views

A tree view represents a set of hierarchical data in the form of an indented outline, which users can expand and collapse. Tree views are useful for displaying data such as the folders and files in a file system or the table of contents in a help system.

A tree view consists of nodes. The top-level node, from which all other nodes branch, is the root node. Nodes that might have subnodes are called "containers." All other nodes are called "leaves." The default icon for a container is a folder, and the default icon for a leaf is a file. Each node is accompanied by text.

Turners appear next to each container in the tree view. The **turner** points right when the container is collapsed and down when the container is expanded.

In the following figure, the Projects, Fire station, First floor, and Landscaping nodes are expanded containers; all the other containers are collapsed. Landscaping is a container without subnodes. Communications, Garage, and Shop are leaves. The turner, container, and leaf graphics shown in this figure are the default graphics provided by the JFC.

FIGURE 167 Tree View With Top-Level Lines

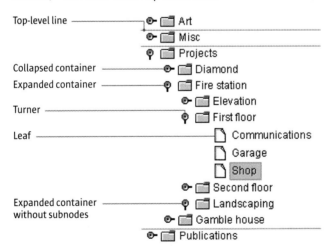

Users can click the right-pointing turner to expand a container so that its contents are visible in the tree view. The turner rotates to point downward. Clicking the downward-pointing turner collapses a container so that its contents are no longer visible. For the keyboard operations that are appropriate for tree views, see Table 32 on page 203.

☕ In most tree views, display the second level of the hierarchy as your highest level. Your outline will be easier to use if you do not display the root node.

☕ Display turners for all containers in the tree view, including the containers at the highest level. Turners remind users that they can expand and collapse the node.

▦▭ Setting the `rootVisible` property of the tree view to false turns off the display of the root node.

▦▭ Setting the `showsRootHandles` of the tree view to true turns on the display of turners for the highest-level containers.

Lines in Tree Views

The JFC provides you three options for including lines in a tree view. The first option is not to include any lines. The second option is to draw lines that separate the top-level nodes, as shown in Figure 167 on page 187. The third option is to draw lines that define the hierarchical relationships of the nodes, as shown in the following figure.

FIGURE 168 Tree View With Hierarchy Lines

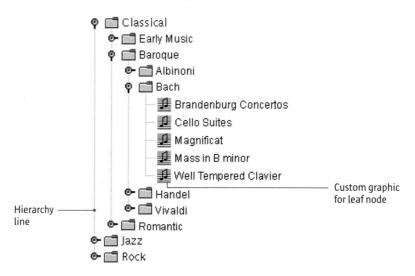

▦▭ The client property `JTree.lineStyle` can be set to `None` to display no lines, to `Horizontal` to display top-level lines, and to `Angled` to display hierarchy lines.

Graphics in Tree Views   You can substitute your own graphics for the JFC-supplied container and leaf node graphics. For example, if your hierarchy represents the clients and servers in a network, you might include graphic representations of the clients and servers. In Figure 168 on page 188, a custom music graphic is used for the leaf nodes. You might also use separate graphics to show when a container is expanded and when it is collapsed.

Editing in Tree Views   You can enable users to edit the text in a tree view. When editing is enabled, users can change text using the same editing commands that they use for text fields. These commands are described in "Editable Text Fields" on page 167.

⊞⊃ Setting the `editable` property to true enables editing of all nodes in the tree.

A: KEYBOARD NAVIGATION, ACTIVATION, AND SELECTION

This appendix defines the keyboard operations that enable users to navigate through, activate, or select the JFC user interface components. (Navigating means to move the input focus from one user interface component to another; activating refers to operating the component; selecting means to choose one or more components, typically for a subsequent action.) For an overview of these concepts, see "Keyboard Navigation and Activation" on page 85.

In general, navigating between components uses these keys:

- **Tab.** Moves keyboard focus to the next component or to the first member of the next group of components.

- **Ctrl-Tab.** Moves keyboard focus to the next component or to the first member of a group of components when the current component accepts a tab (as in text fields, tables, and tabbed panes).

- **Shift-Tab.** Moves keyboard focus to the previous component or to the first component in the previous group of components.

- **Arrow keys.** Move keyboard focus within the individual components of a group of components—for example, within menu items in a menu or within tabs in a tabbed pane.

This appendix presents the JFC-supplied keyboard navigation, activation, and selection operations in a series of tables, arranged alphabetically by component. The left column of each table describes an action (for example, moving focus to the left) and the right column describes its keyboard operation (for example, left arrow key).

Some actions in the table list several possible keyboard operations, separated by a comma. For example, both Home and Ctrl-Home move focus to the beginning of a list. Multiple operations take into account the differences between the Microsoft Windows and CDE operating environments. If you are using an environment other than the Microsoft Windows or CDE operating environment, implement the keyboard operation that is most appropriate for your environment.

⊟⊃ Some of the keyboard operations described in the following tables might be temporarily incomplete or not implemented. However, these key sequences should be reserved for future versions of the JFC and the Java 2 platform.

Checkboxes
The following table lists the keyboard operation for checkboxes. For more information on this component, see "Checkboxes" on page 154.

TABLE 13   Keyboard Operation for Checkboxes

Action	Keyboard Operation
Selects or deselects checkbox	Spacebar

Combo Boxes
The following table lists the keyboard operations for combo boxes. For details on this component, see "Combo Boxes" on page 156.

TABLE 14   Keyboard Operations for Combo Boxes

Action	Keyboard Operation
Posts associated list	Spacebar, down arrow, Alt-down arrow
Closes associated list	Escape
Selects highlighted item and closes list	Enter, Return, spacebar
Moves highlight within list when menu is posted	Up arrow, down arrow

Command Buttons

The following table lists the keyboard operations for command buttons. For more information on this component, see "Command Buttons" on page 148.

TABLE 15   Keyboard Operations for Command Buttons

Action	Keyboard Operation
Activates command button	Spacebar
Activates default button (does not require keyboard focus)	Enter, Return
Activates Cancel button (does not require keyboard focus)	Escape

Desktop Panes and Internal Frames

The following table lists the keyboard operations for desktop panes and internal frames. For details on internal frames and desktop panes, see "Working With Multiple Document Interfaces" on page 108.

TABLE 16   Keyboard Operations for Desktop Panes and Internal Frames

Action	Keyboard Operation
Opens internal frame	Ctrl-F5
Closes internal frame	Ctrl-F4
Moves internal frame	Ctrl-F7
Resizes internal frame	Ctrl-F8
Minimizes internal frame	Ctrl-F9
Navigates first between open internal frames, then among minimized internal frames	Ctrl-Esc, Ctrl-Tab, Shift-Esc, Shift-Tab
Opens minimized internal frame that has keyboard focus	Ctrl-F5, Enter, Return

TABLE 16   Keyboard Operations for Desktop Panes and Internal Frames *(Continued)*

Action	Keyboard Operation
Navigates among associated windows on the desktop pane	Ctrl-F6, Shift-Ctrl-F6
Navigates between associated windows when an internal frame creates a secondary window	Ctrl-F6, Shift-Ctrl-F6
Displays desktop contextual menu	Ctrl-spacebar

Dialog Boxes

The following table lists the keyboard operations for dialog boxes, alert boxes, and utility windows. For comprehensive treatment of dialog boxes and alert boxes, see Chapter 8. For a discussion of utility windows, see "Utility Windows" on page 100.

TABLE 17   Keyboard Operations for Dialog Boxes

Action	Keyboard Operation
Navigates into dialog box	Alt-F6
Navigates out of dialog box	Alt-F6
Activates Cancel button	Escape
Activates default command button	Enter, Return

HTML Editor Kits

HTML editor kits use the navigation, selection, and activation sequences described in Table 27 on page 200, plus the two listed here. For details on the appearance and behavior of this component, see "HTML Editor Kit" on page 172.

TABLE 18   Keyboard Operations for HTML Panes

Action	Keyboard Operation
Navigates to link and other focusable elements	Tab, Shift-Tab, Ctrl-Tab, Shift-Ctrl-Tab
Activates link	Enter, Return, spacebar

Lists

The actions listed in the following table assume multiple selection in lists. For more information on the appearance, behavior, and selection of this component, see "Lists" on page 173.

TABLE 19   Keyboard Operations for Lists

Action	Keyboard Operation
Moves focus up one row or line	Up arrow
Moves focus down one row or line	Down arrow
Moves focus up one view minus one line, giving focus to first line in the view	Page Up
Moves focus down one view minus one line, giving focus to first line in the view	Page Down
Moves focus to beginning of list	Home, Ctrl-Home
Moves focus to end of list	End, Ctrl-End
Selects all items in list	Ctrl-A, Ctrl-/
Deselects all	Ctrl-/
Makes a selection (and deselects any previous selection)	Spacebar
Toggles selection (and does not affect previous selections)	Ctrl-spacebar
Extends selection	Shift-spacebar
Extends selection down one item	Shift-down arrow
Extends selection up one item	Shift-up arrow
Extends selection to beginning of list	Shift-Home
Extends selection to end of list	Shift-End
Extends selection up one view	Shift-PgUp
Extends selection down one view	Shift-PgDn

Menus

The keyboard operations in this table apply to menu bars, menus, drop-down menus, submenus, contextual menus, menu items, radio button menu items, and checkbox menu items. For a discussion of menus, see Chapter 9.

TABLE 20   Keyboard Operations for Menus

Action	Keyboard Operation
Posts current menu	Enter, Return, spacebar, arrow keys
Dismisses menu without taking action and returns focus to last component that had focus	Escape
Moves focus to menu bar and posts first menu	F10
Navigates within menus	Arrow keys
Navigates between titles in menu bar	Arrow keys
Activates a menu item, dismisses menu, and goes to last window item with focus	Enter, Return, spacebar
Displays contextual menu	Shift-F10
Dismisses contextual menu	Escape
Navigates within contextual menu	Arrow keys
Activates highlighted item in contextual menu and dismisses menu	Enter, Return, spacebar

Radio Buttons

The following table lists the keyboard operation for radio buttons. For a discussion of the appearance and behavior of this component, see "Radio Buttons" on page 155.

TABLE 21   Keyboard Operation for Radio Buttons

Action	Keyboard Operation
Selects radio button	Spacebar

Scrollbars

Users can operate scrollbars from the keyboard when keyboard focus is anywhere in the scroll pane that contains the scrollbar. For a discussion of the appearance and behavior of this component, see "Scrollbars" on page 102.

TABLE 22   Keyboard Operations for Scrollbars

Action	Keyboard Operation
Moves view up one line	Up arrow
Moves view down one line	Down arrow
Moves up one view	Page Up
Moves down one view	Page Down
Moves to beginning of data	Ctrl-Home
Moves to end of data	Ctrl-End
Moves right one view minus one line	Ctrl-PgDn
Moves left one view	Ctrl-Pg Up

Sliders

The following table lists the keyboard operations for sliders. For details on this component, see "Sliders" on page 159.

TABLE 23   Keyboard Operations for Sliders

Action	Keyboard Operation
Changes value of slider	Arrow keys
Moves to left/top value	Home
Moves to right/bottom value	End
Jumps in left/top direction (approximately 20% of the scale)	Page Up, Ctrl-PgUp
Jumps in right/bottom direction (approximately 20% of the scale)	Page Down, Ctrl-PgDn

Split Panes
The following table lists the keyboard operations for split panes. After users enter a split pane, pressing Tab cycles the focus to the components within the split pane. For a description of the appearance and behavior of this component, see "Split Panes" on page 106.

TABLE 24   Keyboard Operations for Split Panes

Action	Keyboard Operation
Navigates between split panes and gives focus to last element that had focus	Tab, F6
Gives focus to splitter bar	F8
Changes location of splitter bar in splitter pane	Arrow keys, Home, End

Tabbed Panes
The following table lists the keyboard operations for tabbed panes. For a description of the appearance and behavior of this component, see "Tabbed Panes" on page 104. When a tabbed pane initially gets focus, the focus goes to one of the tabs, and not to one of the content panes.

TABLE 25   Keyboard Operations for Tabbed Panes

Action	Keyboard Operation
Navigates through tabs	Arrow keys
Moves from tab to its associated content pane	Ctrl-down arrow
Moves from content pane to its associated tab	Ctrl-up arrow
Moves to next or previous content pane	Ctrl-PgDn or Ctrl-PgUp

Tables

The following table lists the keyboard operations for tables. For a description of the appearance and behavior of this component, see "Tables" on page 176.

TABLE 26   Keyboard Operations for Tables

Action	Keyboard Operations
Moves focus up one cell	Shift-Return
Moves focus down one cell	Return
Moves focus left one cell	Shift-Tab
Moves focus right one cell	Tab
Deselects current selection and moves focus up one cell	Up arrow
Deselects current selection and moves focus down one cell	Down arrow
Scrolls up one view and gives focus to first visible cell in the current column	Page Up
Scrolls down one view and gives focus to first visible cell in the current column	Page Down
Scrolls left one view and gives focus to first visible cell in the current row	Ctrl-PgUp
Scrolls right one view and gives focus to first visible cell in the current row	Ctrl-PgDn
Moves focus and view to first cell in the current row	Home
Moves focus and view to last cell in the current row	End
Moves focus and view to first cell in the current column	Ctrl-Home
Moves focus and view to last cell in the current column	Ctrl-End
Allows editing in a cell without overwriting the information	F2
Resets cell to the state it was in before it was edited	Escape
Selects entire table	Ctrl-A

TABLE 26   Keyboard Operations for Tables *(Continued)*

Action	Keyboard Operations
Extends selection up one row	Shift-up arrow
Extends selection down one row	Shift-down arrow
Extends selection left one column	Shift-left arrow
Extends selection right one column	Shift-down arrow
Extends selection to beginning of row	Shift-Home
Extends selection to end of row	Shift-End
Extends selection to beginning of column	Ctrl-Shift-Home
Extends selection to end of column	Ctrl-Shift-End
Extends selection up one view	Shift-PgUp
Extends selection down one view	Shift-PgDn
Extends selection left one view	Ctrl-Shift-PgUp
Extends selection right one view	Ctrl-Shift-PgDn

Text Areas and Default and Styled Text Editor Kits

The following table lists the keyboard operations for text areas and the default and styled text editor kits. For details on the appearance and behavior of these components, see "Text Areas" on page 169, "Default Editor Kit" on page 170, and "Styled Text Editor Kit" on page 170.

TABLE 27   Keyboard Operations for Text Areas and Default and Styled Text Editor Kits

Action	Keyboard Operation
Moves insertion point up one line	Up arrow
Moves insertion point down one line	Down arrow
Moves insertion point to the left one component or character	Left arrow
Moves insertion point to the right one component or character	Right arrow
Moves up one view	Page Up
Moves down one view	Page Down

TABLE 27 Keyboard Operations for Text Areas and Default and Styled Text Editor
Kits *(Continued)*

Action	Keyboard Operation
Moves left one view	Ctrl-PgUp
Moves right one view	Ctrl-PgDn
Moves to beginning of line	Home
Moves to end of row or line	End
Moves to beginning of data	Ctrl-Home
Moves to end of data	Ctrl-End
Moves to next word	Ctrl-right arrow
Moves to previous word	Ctrl-left arrow
Selects all	Ctrl-A, Ctrl-/
Deselects all	Ctrl-\
Extends selection up	Shift-up arrow
Extends selection down	Shift-down arrow
Extends selection left	Shift-left arrow
Extends selection right	Shift-right arrow
Extends selection up one view	Shift-PgUp
Extends selection down one view	Shift-PgDown
Extends selection to the left one view	Ctrl-Shift-PgUp
Extends selection to the right one view	Ctrl-Shift-PgDn
Extends selection to beginning of line	Shift-Home
Extends selection to end of line	Shift-End
Extends selection to beginning of data	Ctrl-Shift-Home
Extends selection to end of data	Ctrl-Shift-End
Extends selection to next word	Ctrl-Shift-right arrow
Extends selection to previous word	Ctrl-Shift-left arrow

Text Fields

The following table lists the keyboard operations for text fields. For details on this component, see "Text Fields" on page 167.

TABLE 28   Keyboard Operations for Text Fields

Action	Keyboard Operation
Moves insertion point one character to the right	Right arrow
Moves insertion point one character to the left	Left arrow
Moves insertion point to beginning of next word	Ctrl-right arrow
Moves insertion point to beginning of previous word	Ctrl-left arrow
Moves insertion point to beginning of field	Home
Moves insertion point to end of field	End
Submits text entry	Enter, Return
Extends selection to beginning of line	Shift-Home
Extends selection to end of line	Shift-End
Extends selection one character to the left	Shift-left arrow
Extends selection one character to the right	Shift-right arrow
Extends selection to next word	Shift-Ctrl-right arrow
Extends selection to previous word	Shift-Ctrl-left arrow

Toggle Buttons

The following table lists the keyboard operation for toggle buttons. For details on this component, see "Toggle Buttons" on page 152.

TABLE 29   Keyboard Operation for Toggle Buttons

Action	Keyboard Operation
Toggles button on or off	Spacebar

Tool Tips

The following table lists the keyboard operations for tool tips. For details on this component, see "Tool Tips" on page 145.

TABLE 30   Keyboard Operations for Tool Tips

Action	Keyboard Operation
Displays tool tip	Ctrl-F1
Removes tool tip	Escape, Ctrl-F1

Toolbars

The following table lists the keyboard operations for toolbars. For details on the appearance and behavior of this component, see "Toolbars" on page 140.

TABLE 31   Keyboard Operations for Toolbars

Action	Keyboard Operation
Navigates within toolbar	Arrow keys
Activates toolbar	Spacebar

Tree Views

The following table lists the keyboard operations for tree views. For details on the appearance and behavior of this component, see "Tree Views" on page 187.

TABLE 32   Keyboard Operations for Tree Views

Action	Keyboard Operation
Expands current node	Right arrow
Collapses current node	Left arrow
Moves focus up one node	Up arrow
Moves focus down one node	Down arrow
Moves focus to first node in tree	Home
Moves focus to last node in tree	End
Moves up one view	Page Up
Moves down one view	Page Down

TABLE 32   Keyboard Operations for Tree Views *(Continued)*

Action	Keyboard Operation
Moves left one view	Ctrl-PgUp
Moves right one view	Ctrl-PgDn
Selects all nodes in tree	Ctrl-A, Ctrl-/
Deselects all	Ctrl-\
Extends selection down	Shift-down arrow
Extends selection up	Shift-up arrow
Extends selection to beginning of tree	Shift-Home
Extends selection to end of tree	Shift-End
Extends selection up one view	Shift-PgUp
Extends selection down one view	Shift-PgDn
Extends selection right one view	Ctrl-Shift-PgDn
Extends selection left one view	Ctrl-Shift-PgUp

GLOSSARY

Abstract Window Toolkit

The class library that provides the standard API for building GUIs for Java programs. The Abstract Window Toolkit (AWT) includes imaging tools, data transfer classes, GUI components, containers for GUI components, an event system for handling user and system events among parts of the AWT, and layout managers for managing the size and position of GUI components in platform-independent designs. (The GUI components in the AWT are implemented as native-platform versions of the components, and they have largely been supplanted by the Swing components.) See also **Java Foundation Classes**, **Swing classes**.

accessibility

The degree to which software can be used comfortably by a wide variety of people, including those who require assistive technologies like screen magnifiers or voice recognition. An accessible JFC application employs the Java Accessibility API, enables its users to select an appropriate look and feel, and provides keyboard operations for all actions that can be carried out by use of the mouse. See also **Java Accessibility API**, **Java Accessibility Utilities**, **keyboard operations**.

alert box

A dialog box used by an application to convey a message or warning or to gather information from the user. Four standard alert boxes (Question, Info, Error, and Warning) are supplied for JFC applications. Alert boxes are created using the JOptionPane component. See also **dialog box**.

applet

A program, written in the Java language, that a user can interact with in a web browser. See also **application**.

application

A program that combines all the functions necessary for a user to accomplish a particular set of tasks (for instance, word processing or inventory tracking). Unless stated otherwise, this book uses "application" to refer to both applets and standalone applications. See also **applet**.

assistive technology   Hardware or software that helps people with disabilities use a computer (or provides alternative means of use to all users). Examples include pointing devices other than the mouse, audio or text-only browsers, and screen readers that translate the contents of the screen into Braille, voice output, or audible cues.

AWT   See **Abstract Window Toolkit.**

bit depth   The amount of information (in bits) used to represent a pixel. A bit depth of 8 supports up to 256 colors; a bit depth of 24 supports up to 16,777,216 colors.

browser   An application that enables users to view, navigate through, and interact with HTML documents and applets. Also called a "web browser."

button   A collective term for the various controls whose on-screen appearance typically simulates a push button or a radio button. The user clicks buttons to specify commands or set options. See also **checkbox, command button, radio button, toggle button, toolbar button.**

checkbox   A control, consisting of a graphic and associated text, that a user clicks to select or deselect an option. A check mark in the checkbox graphic indicates that the option is selected. Checkboxes are created using the JCheckBox component. See also **radio button.**

checkbox menu item   A menu item that appears with a checkbox next to it to represent an on or off setting. A check mark in the checkbox graphic indicates that the menu item is selected. Checkbox menu items are created using the JCheckBoxMenuItem component. See also **menu item.**

color chooser   A component that enables a user to select a color. Color choosers are created using the JColorChooser component. See also **HSB, palette window, RGB, utility window.**

combo box   A component with a drop-down arrow that the user clicks to display a list of options. Noneditable combo boxes (sometimes called "list boxes") have a list from which the user can select one item. Editable combo boxes offer a text field as well as a list of options. The user can make a selection by typing a value in the text field or by selecting an item from the list. Combo boxes are created using the JComboBox component.

command button   A button with a rectangular border that contains text, a graphic, or both. A user clicks a command button to specify a command to initiate an action. Command buttons are created using the `JButton` component. See also **button**, **toggle button**, **toolbar button**.

component   A piece of code or, by extension, the interface element implemented by that code. See also **Swing classes**.

container   A component (such as an applet, window, pane, or internal frame) that holds other components.

contextual menu   A menu that is displayed when a user presses mouse button 2 while the pointer is over an object or area associated with that menu. A contextual menu offers only menu items that are applicable to the object or region at the location of the pointer. Sometimes called a "pop-up menu." Contextual menus are created using the `JPopupMenu` component. See also **menu**.

control   An interface element that a user can manipulate to perform an action, select an option, or set a value. Examples include buttons, sliders, and combo boxes.

cross-platform   Pertaining to heterogeneous computing environments. For example, a cross-platform application is one that has a single code base for multiple operating systems.

cursor   See **pointer**.

default command button   The command button that the application activates if a user presses Enter or Return. Default buttons in Java look and feel applications have a heavier border than other command buttons. See also **command button**.

designer   A professional who specifies the way that users will interact with an application, chooses the interface components, and lays them out in a set of views. The designer might or might not be the same person as the developer who writes the application code.

desktop pane   A container, a sort of "virtual desktop," for an MDI application. Desktop panes are created using the `JDesktopPane` component. See also **internal frame**, **MDI**.

dialog box   A secondary window displayed by an application to gather information from users or to inform them of a condition. A dialog box can contain panes, lists, buttons, and other components. Dialog boxes are created using the JDialog component. See also **alert box**, **color chooser**, **palette window**, **secondary window**, **utility window**.

dithering   Simulating unavailable colors in a displayed graphic by using a pattern of two or more available colors.

drag   To move the mouse while holding down a mouse button. See also **drag and drop**.

drag and drop   To drag an interface element to a new location in order to move, copy, or link it. See also **drag**.

drop-down arrow   The triangular indicator that a user clicks to view more options than are visible on screen—such as the list attached to a combo box or the options provided by some toolbar buttons.

drop-down menu   A menu that is displayed when a user chooses a menu title in the menu bar. Drop-down menus are created using the JMenu component. See also **menu**, **menu bar**.

editor pane   A component that supports a variety of plug-in editor kits. The JFC includes editor kits that can display plain, styled, HTML, and RTF data. Editor panes are created using the JEditorPane component. See also **plug-in editor kit**.

flush 3D style   In the Java look and feel, the effect created by rendering on-screen graphics whose surfaces appear to be in the same plane as the surrounding canvas.

GIF   Graphics Interchange Format. An 8-bit graphics format developed by CompuServe and commonly used on the World Wide Web. GIF files are limited to 256 colors, and they compress without loss of information. The GIF format is typically used for graphics in the Java look and feel. See also **bit depth**, **JPEG**.

HSB   For "hue, saturation, brightness." In computer graphics, a color model in which hue refers to a color's light frequency, saturation is the amount or strength of the hue (its purity), and brightness is the amount of black in the color (its lightness or darkness). See also **RGB**.

icon   An on-screen graphic representing an interface element that a user can select or manipulate—for example, an application, document, or disk.

insertion point

The place, usually indicated by a blinking bar, where typed text or a dragged or pasted selection will appear. See also **pointer**.

internal frame

A container used in MDI applications to create windows that a user cannot drag outside of the desktop pane. In an MDI application that uses the Java look and feel, internal frames have a window border, title bar, and standard window controls with the Java look and feel. Internal frames are created using the `JInternalFrame` component. See also **desktop pane, MDI**.

internationalization

The process of preparing software that is suitable for the global marketplace, taking into account wide variations in regions, languages, and cultures. Internationalization usually requires the separation of component text from code to ease the process of translation. See also **localization**.

Java 2D API

A programming interface (part of the Java Foundation Classes in the Java 2 SDK) that provides an advanced two-dimensional imaging model for complex shapes, text, and images. Features include enhanced font and color support and a single, comprehensive rendering model. See also **Java Foundation Classes**.

Java 2 SDK

The software development kit that developers need to build applications for the Java 2 Platform, Standard Edition, v. 1.2. See also **Java Development Kit**.

Java Accessibility API

A programming interface (part of the Java Foundation Classes) that enables assistive technologies to interact and communicate with JFC components. A Java application that fully supports the Java Accessibility API is compatible with such technologies as screen readers and screen magnifiers. See also **accessibility, assistive technology, Java Accessibility Utilities, Java Foundation Classes**.

Java Accessibility Utilities

A set of classes (provided in the Java 2 SDK) for use by the vendors who create assistive technologies or automated tool tests. See also **accessibility, assistive technology, Java Accessibility API, Java Foundation Classes**.

Java Development Kit

Software that includes the APIs and tools that developers need to build applications for those versions of the Java platform that preceded the Java 2 Platform. Also called the "JDK." See also **Java 2 SDK**.

Java Foundation Classes	A product that includes the Swing classes, pluggable look and feel designs, and the Java Accessibility API (all implemented without native code and compatible with JDK 1.1). For the Java 2 platform, the Java Foundation Classes (JFC) also include the Java 2D API, drag and drop, and other enhancements. See also **Abstract Window Toolkit, pluggable look and feel architecture, Swing classes.**
Java look and feel	The default appearance and behavior for JFC applications, designed for cross-platform use. The Java look and feel works in the same way on any platform that supports the Java Foundation Classes. See also **Java Foundation Classes, pluggable look and feel architecture.**
JDK	See **Java Development Kit.**
JFC	See **Java Foundation Classes.**
JFC application	An application built with the Java Foundation Classes. See also **Java Foundation Classes.**
JPEG	A graphics format developed by the Joint Photographic Experts Group. The JPEG format is frequently used for photographs and other complex images that benefit from a larger color palette than a GIF image can provide. JPEG compression is "lossy"; decompressed images are not identical to uncompressed images. See also **GIF.**
keyboard focus	The active window or component where the user's next keystrokes will take effect. Sometimes called the "input focus."
keyboard operations	A collective term for keyboard shortcuts, mnemonics, and other forms of navigation and activation that utilize the keyboard instead of the mouse. See also **keyboard shortcut, mnemonic.**
keyboard shortcut	A keystroke combination (usually a modifier key and a character key, like Control-C) that activates a menu item from the keyboard even if the relevant menu is not currently displayed. See also **keyboard operations, mnemonic.**
label	Static text that appears in the interface. For example, a label might identify a group of checkboxes. (The text that accompanies each checkbox within the group, however, is specified in the individual checkbox component and is therefore not considered a label.) Labels are created using the `JLabel` component.

layout manager   An object that assists the designer in determining the size and position of components within a container. Each container type has a default layout manager. See also **Abstract Window Toolkit**.

list   A set of choices from which a user can select one or more items. Items in a list can be text, graphics, or both. Lists are created using the JList component. See also **combo box**.

localization   The process of customizing software for a particular locale. Localization usually involves translation and often requires changes to fonts, keyboard usage, and date and time formats. See also **internationalization**.

look and feel   The appearance and behavior of a complete set of GUI components. See also **Java look and feel**.

MDI   Multiple document interface. An interface that confines all of an application's internal frames inside its desktop pane. See also **desktop pane**.

menu   A list of choices (menu items) logically grouped and displayed by an application so that a user need not memorize all available commands or options. Menus in the Java look and feel are "sticky"—that is, they remain posted on screen after the user clicks the menu title. Menus are created using the JMenu component. See also **contextual menu, drop-down menu, menu bar, menu item, submenu**.

menu bar   The horizontal strip at the top of a window that contains the titles of the application's drop-down menus. Menu bars are created using the JMenuBar component. See also **drop-down menu**.

menu item   A choice in a menu. Menu items (text or graphics) are typically commands or other options that a user can select. Menu items are created using the JMenuItem component. See also **checkbox menu item, radio button menu item**.

middle mouse button The central button on a three-button mouse (typically used in UNIX environments). The Java look and feel does not utilize the middle mouse button. See also **mouse button 2**.

MIME   Multipurpose Internet Mail Extensions. An Internet standard for sending and receiving non-ASCII email attachments (including video, audio, and graphics). Web browsers also use MIME types to assign applications interpret and display files that are not written in HTML.

minimized internal frame
A reduced representation of an internal frame in an MDI application. Minimized internal frames look like horizontally oriented tags that appear at the lower-left corner of the desktop. The user can drag minimized internal frames to rearrange them. See also **MDI**.

mnemonic
An underlined letter, typically in a menu title, menu item, or the text of a button or component. A mnemonic shows the user which key to press (in conjunction with the Alt key) to activate a command or navigate to a component. See also **keyboard operations**, **keyboard shortcut**.

modal dialog box
In a JFC application, a dialog box that prevents the user's interaction with other windows in the current application. Modal dialog boxes are created using the JDialog component. See also **dialog box**, **modeless dialog box**.

modeless dialog box
In a JFC application, a dialog box whose presence does not prevent the user from interacting with other windows in the current application. Modeless dialog boxes are created using the JDialog component. See also **dialog box**, **modal dialog box**.

modifier key
A key (for example, the Control or the Shift key) that does not produce an alphanumeric character but rather modifies the action of other keys.

mouse button 1
The primary button on a mouse (the only button, for Macintosh users). By default, mouse button 1 is the leftmost button, though users might switch the button settings so that the rightmost button becomes mouse button 1. See also **middle mouse button**, **mouse button 2**.

mouse button 2
On a two-button or three-button mouse, the button that is used to display contextual menus. By default, mouse button 2 is the rightmost button on the mouse, though users might switch the settings so that the leftmost button becomes mouse button 2. See also **contextual menu**, **middle mouse button**, **mouse button 1**.

mouse-over feedback
A change in the visual appearance of an interface element that occurs when the user moves the pointer over it—for example, the display of a button border when the pointer moves over a toolbar button.

multiple document interface
See **MDI**.

native code   Code that refers to the methods of a specific operating system or is compiled for a specific processor.

palette window   In an MDI application with the Java look and feel, a modeless window that displays a collection of tools, colors, or patterns. Palette windows float on top of document windows. User choices made in a palette window affect whichever primary window is active. Palette windows are created using the JInternalFrame component. See also **utility window**.

pane   A collective term for scroll panes, split panes, and tabbed panes.

panel   A container for organizing the contents of a window, dialog box, or applet. Panels are created using the JPanel component. See also **tabbed pane**.

password field   A special text field in which the user types a password. The field displays a masking character for each typed character. Password fields are created using the JPasswordField component.

plain window   An unadorned window with no title bar or window controls, typically used for splash screens. Plain windows are created using the JWindow component. See also **primary window**, **window controls**.

pluggable look and feel architecture   An architecture that separates the implementation of interface elements from their presentation, enabling an application to dynamically choose how its interface elements interact with users. When a pluggable look and feel is used for an application, the designer can select from several look and feel designs.

plug-in editor kit   An editor that can be used by the editor pane. The Java Foundation Classes supply plug-in editor kits for plain, styled, RTF, and HTML data.

pointer   A small graphic that moves around the screen as the user manipulates the mouse (or another pointing device). Depending on its location and the active application, the pointer can assume various shapes, such as an arrowhead, crosshair, or clock. By moving the pointer and pressing mouse buttons, a user can select objects, set the insertion point, and activate windows. Sometimes called the "cursor." See also **insertion point**.

preference   A setting for an application or tool. Typically set by users. See also **property**.

primary window	A top-level window of an application, where the principal interaction with the user occurs. Primary windows always retain the look and feel of the user's native platform. Primary windows are created using the `JFrame` component. See also **dialog box**, **secondary window**.
progress bar	An interface element that indicates one or more operations are in progress and shows the user what proportion of the operations has been completed. Progress bars are created using the `JProgressBar` component. See also **control, slider**.
property	A characteristic of an object. Depending on the object, the user or the designer might set its properties. See also **preference**.
radio button	A button that a user clicks to set an option. Unlike checkboxes, radio buttons are mutually exclusive—selecting one radio button deselects all other radio buttons in the group. Radio buttons are created using the `JRadioButton` component. See also **checkbox**.
radio button menu item	A menu item that appears with a radio button next to it. Separators indicate which radio button menu items are in a group. Selecting one radio button menu item deselects all others in that group. Radio button menu items are created using the `JRadioButtonMenuItem` component.
resource bundle	The place where an application stores its locale-specific data (isolated from source code).
RGB	For "red, green, blue." In computer graphics, a color model that represents colors as percentages of red, green, and blue. See also **HSB**.
scroll arrow	In a scrollbar, one of the arrows that a user can click to move through displayed information in the corresponding direction (up or down in a vertical scrollbar, left or right in a horizontal scrollbar). See also **scrollbar**.
scroll box	A box that a user can drag in the channel of a scrollbar to cause scrolling in the corresponding direction. The scroll box's position in the scrollbar indicates the user's location in the list, window, or pane. In the Java look and feel, the scroll box's size indicates what proportion of the total information is currently visible on screen. A large scroll box, for example, indicates that the user can peruse the contents with just a few clicks in the scrollbar. See also **scrollbar**.

scroll pane   A container that provides scrolling with optional vertical and horizontal scrollbars. Scroll panes are created using the JScrollPane component. See also **scrollbar**.

scrollbar   A component that enables a user to control what portion of a document or list (or similar information) is visible on screen. A scrollbar consists of a vertical or horizontal channel, a scroll box that moves through the channel of the scrollbar, and two scroll arrows. Scrollbars are created using the JScrollBar component. See also **scroll arrow, scroll box, scroll pane**.

secondary window   A modal or modeless window created from and dependent upon a primary window. Secondary windows set options or supply additional details about actions and objects in the primary window. Secondary windows are dismissed when their associated primary window is dismissed. Secondary windows are created using either the JFrame or the JDialog component. See also **dialog box, primary window**.

separator   A line graphic that is used to divide menu items into logical groupings. Separators are created using the JSeparator component.

slider   A control that enables the user to set a value in a range—for example, the RGB values for a color. Sliders are created using the JSlider component. See also **progress bar**.

split pane   A container that enables the user to adjust the relative size of two adjacent panes. Split panes are created using the JSplitPane component.

submenu   A menu that is displayed when a user chooses a certain menu item in a higher-level menu. Submenus are created using the JMenu component.

Swing classes   A set of GUI components, featuring a pluggable look and feel, that are included in the Java Foundation Classes. The Swing classes implement the Java Accessibility API and supply code for interface elements such as windows, dialog boxes and choosers, panels and panes, menus, controls, text components, tables, lists, and tree views. See also **Abstract Window Toolkit, Java Foundation Classes, pluggable look and feel architecture**.

tabbed pane   A container that enables the user to switch between several components (usually JPanel components) that appear to share the same space on screen. The user can view a particular panel by clicking its tab. Tabbed panes are created using the JTabbedPane component.

table
A two-dimensional arrangement of data in rows and columns. Tables are created using the `JTable` component.

text area
A multiline region for displaying (and sometimes editing) text. Text in such areas is restricted to a single font, size, and style. Text areas are created using the `JTextArea` component. See also **editor pane**.

text field
An area that displays a single line of text. In a noneditable text field, a user can copy, but not change, the text. In an editable text field, a user can type new text or edit the existing text. Text fields are created using the `JTextField` component. See also **password field**.

theme mechanism
A feature that enables a designer to specify alternative colors and fonts across an entire Java look and feel application. See also **Java look and feel**.

title bar
The strip at the top of a window that contains its title and window controls. See also **window controls**.

toggle button
A button that alternates between two states. For example, a user might click one toggle button in a toolbar to turn italics on and off. A single toggle button has checkbox behavior; a programmatically grouped set of toggle buttons can be given the mutually exclusive behavior of radio buttons. Toggle buttons are created using the `JToggleButton` component. See also **toolbar button**.

tool tip
A short text string that appears on screen to describe the interface element beneath the pointer.

toolbar
A collection of frequently used commands or options. Toolbars typically contain buttons, but other components (such as text fields and combo boxes) can be placed in toolbars as well. Toolbars are created using the `JToolBar` component. See also **toolbar button**.

toolbar button
A button that appears in a toolbar, typically a command or toggle button. Toolbar buttons are created using the `JButton` or `JToggleButton` component. See also **command button**, **toggle button**.

top-level container
The highest-level container for a Java application or applet. The top-level containers are `JWindow`, `JFrame`, and `JDialog`.

tree view   A representation of hierarchical data (for example, directory and file names) as a graphical outline. Clicking expands or collapses elements of the outline. Tree views are created using the `JTree` component.

turner   A graphic used in the tree view component. The user clicks a turner to expand or collapse a container in the hierarchy.

utility window   In a non-MDI application with the Java look and feel, a modeless dialog box that typically displays a collection of tools, colors, fonts, or patterns. Unlike palette windows, utility windows do not float. User choices made in a utility window affect whichever primary window is active. A utility window is not dismissed when a primary window is dismissed. Utility windows are created using the `JDialog` component. See also **palette window, secondary window.**

web browser   See **browser.**

window   See **dialog box, palette window, plain window, primary window, secondary window, utility window.**

window controls   Controls that affect the state of a window (for example, the Maximize button in Microsoft Windows title bars).

INDEX

NUMERALS

8-bit colors, 58–62

256-color displays, 58–62

A

About Application item (Help menu), 139

About boxes, 76

Abstract Window Toolkit (AWT), 16

accelerator keys. *See* keyboard shortcuts

access keys. *See* mnemonics

accessibility, 30–32

    ease of use and, 30

    JFC support for, 16–17

    keyboard focus and, 32, 83–85

    mnemonics and, 31–32, 88–90

    multiplexing look and feel, xxv

    recommended reading, xxvii–xxviii

    tab traversal and, 32, 114

    usability tests for, 32

active components, spacing of, 48–49

active windows

    color design for borders, 40, 43

    example, 5

alert boxes, 122–126

    See also dialog boxes

    capitalization of text in, 47

    Error, 124–125

    Info, 123

    keyboard operations for, 194

    platform-specific examples, 10

    Question, 125–126

    Warning, 10, 124

alignment. *See* spacing and alignment

Alt key, 82, 88–89

animation, 54–55

    See also mouse-over feedback

applets, 27–29

    browser windows and, 29

    examples, 5, 10–12

    JFC downloads with, 28

    menus in, 29

    mnemonics in, 29

    recommended reading, xxviii

    security issues, 28–29

application graphics, 57–76

    See also button graphics; colors; icons

    About boxes, 76

    corporate and product identity and, 73–76

    GIF files and, 58–59

    installation screens, 73

    internationalization, 36, 62

    Java look and feel style, 62

    JPEG files and, 58, 73

    splash screens, 73–75

    symbols, 72

    tree views, 189

application windows. *See* primary windows

applications, compared with applets, xix, 5, 27–29

Apply button, 118

arrow keys, 82, 85, 86, 191

arrows. *See* arrow keys; indicators; scroll arrows

assistive technologies, 16–17, 31

    See also accessibility

audience, xix

B

background canvas, color design for, 41, 43

Backspace key, 82

behavioral design, 77–90

bibliography, xxii–xxviii

bit depth, 58

black, use in Java look and feel, 40, 42, 43, 44

blinking. *See* animation

blues, use in Java look and feel, 40–41, 43
borders
    in button graphics, 68, 143–144
    color design for, 43
    in icons, 64
boxes. *See* About boxes; alert boxes; checkboxes;
  combo boxes; dialog boxes
branding, for products, 73–76
browser windows, 5, 10–13, 29
button controls, 147, 148–156
    See also button graphics; checkboxes; command
      buttons; mouse buttons; radio buttons; toggle
      buttons; toolbar buttons
button graphics, 66–72
    See also spacing and alignment
    borders in, 68, 143–144
    drop-down arrows in, 144
    use with text, 45, 142–143, 148, 150

C

Cancel button, 75, 116–117
capitalization, 46–47
cascading menus. *See* submenus
case-sensitivity, in user input, 159
CDE look and feel, 24
cells in tables, 176–177, 180–182
channels (for scrollbars), 103
checkbox menu items, 135
    example, 7
    keyboard operations for, 196
checkboxes, 154–155
    example, 9
    font design for, 45
    keyboard operations for, 192
    in menus, 7, 135
    spacing of, 48–49, 154–155
    text with, 46–47, 154
choosers, color, 126–127
choosing menu items, 133
clicking, 77–78
    See also dragging
    Control-clicking, 80
    double-clicking, 77, 80

    as selection technique, 80
    Shift-clicking, 80
    triple-clicking, 77, 80
client properties, 18
Close button, 76, 116
close controls, 98, 99, 109, 110
    See also window controls
Close item (File menu), 98, 137
collapse box. *See* window controls
color choosers, 126–127
color model, 4, 39–44
colors, 39–44
    See also application graphics
    black, 40, 42, 43, 44
    blues, 40–41, 43
    cross-platform, 57–62
    dithering, 58, 60–62
    graphic file formats and, 58–59
    grays, 40, 42, 43, 44, 60
    Java look and feel model, 39–44
    primary, 40–41, 43–44
    redefining, 44
    secondary, 40, 41–42, 43–44
    table of Java look and feel colors, 43
    web-safe, 58, 60
    white, 40, 42, 43, 44
columns in tables
    reordering, 177
    resizing, 178–179
    selecting, 184–186
combo boxes, 156–159
    capitalization of text with, 46–47
    defined, 147
    editable, 158–159
    example, 9
    internationalization, 36
    keyboard operations for, 192
    noneditable, 157–158
command buttons, 148–150
    See also button graphics; default command
      buttons; toolbar buttons
    in alert boxes, 122–123
    Apply, 118
    Cancel, 75, 116–117

Close, 76, 116
color design for, 41
ellipsis mark in, 150
examples, 8, 9
font design for, 45
Help, 116
keyboard operations for, 193
OK, 116–117
Reset, 118
spacing of, 122–123, 143–144, 151
text with, 46, 142–143, 148, 149, 150–151
Command key, 87
commands, menu. *See* menu items
common menus, 136–139
company logos, 73–76
components, 17–18
spacing between, 47–53
specifying look and feel of, 23–24
table of major JFC components, 19–22
containers, 95–110
See also dialog boxes; windows
content panes, 104–106
contextual menus, 139–140
See also menus
defined, 129
displaying, 80–81
keyboard operations for, 196
Control key, 7, 80, 82–88, 191
control type style, in Java look and feel, 43, 45
controls, 147–161
See also checkboxes; command buttons; radio
buttons; sliders; toggle buttons; window
controls
capitalization of text with, 46–47
in menus, 135–136
copyright information, 74, 76
corporate identity, graphics and, 73–76
crosshair pointers, 79
cross-platform colors, 57–62
See also colors
cross-platform delivery guidelines, defined, xxii
cursors. *See* pointers

D

data loss and alert boxes, 124
default colors, 40–43
See also colors
default command buttons, 149–150
See also command buttons
behavior of, 118–119
examples, 9, 10
mnemonics with, 113
default editor kit, 170, 200–201
default fonts, 45
default pointers, 79
delay feedback, 54–55, 121–122
Delete key, 82
design principles. *See* principles of design
desktop panes, 108–110, 112, 193–194
destination feedback, 82
dialog boxes, 111–127
See also command buttons; spacing and
alignment; utility windows
capitalization of titles and text in, 47
command buttons in, 115–119
find, 120
initial keyboard focus in, 113
international considerations, 35
keyboard operations for, 194
login, 120
mnemonics in, 113
modes, 112
palette windows, 110
platform-specific examples, 8–9
preferences, 9, 113–114, 120–121
print, 121
progress, 54–55, 121–122
tab traversal in, 32, 114
titles for, 113
as top-level containers, 97–99
Dialog font, 45
dimmed text, color design for, 41, 43
disabilities. *See* accessibility
dithering, 58
in button graphics, 71
in icons, 65
prevention of, 60–62

dockable toolbars, 141–142

dots in menus. *See* ellipsis mark

double-clicking, 77, 80

downloading applets, 28

drag texture, 4, 8

drag-and-drop operations, 81–82

dragging
    and dropping, 81–82
    as selection technique, 77, 80
    title bars, 109
    toolbars, 141–142

drop-down arrows
    See also indicators
    for combo boxes, 156–158
    for toolbar buttons, 144

drop-down menus, 131
    See also menus
    common, 136–139
    defined, 129
    displaying, 131
    examples, 6–8
    keyboard operations for, 196
    titles of, 131
    toolbar buttons and, 144

E

ease of use. *See* principles of design

Edit menu, 138
    example, 7
    keyboard shortcuts in, 88
    mnemonics in, 90

editable combo boxes, 158–159
    See also combo boxes
    example, 9
    in login splash screens, 75

editable text fields, 9, 167–168

editing
    password fields, 169
    selection techniques, 77, 80
    tables, 177
    text, 169–172
    text fields, 167–168
    tree views, 189

editor panes, 170–172
    example, 8
    keyboard operations for, 200–201

8-bit colors, 58–62

ellipsis mark
    in command buttons, 150
    in menu items, 134

End key, 82, 87

Enter key, 82, 86, 87, 149

Error alert boxes, 124–125

error messages, 47, 124–125

Escape key, 87, 89, 150

Exit item (File menu), 98, 137

F

Federal Rehabilitation Act, 30

feedback
    animation and, 54–55
    while dragging, 82
    mouse-over, 79, 145
    pointer style as, 54, 78, 82, 106
    progress bars, 160–161
    progress dialog boxes, 54–55, 121–122
    system status, 55

Ferret utility tool, 31

fields. *See* password fields; text fields

File menu, 137
    Close item in, 137
    Exit item in, 137
    keyboard shortcuts in, 88
    mnemonics in, 90
    Preferences item in, 134

find dialog boxes, 120

flush 3D effects
    See also application graphics
    button graphics and, 67, 70
    component spacing and, 48–49
    default theme and, 41, 43
    example, 3
    icons and, 63–64, 65
    symbols and, 62

fonts
> *See also* text
> international considerations, 37
> redefining, 45
> table of default fonts, 45

Format menu, 7, 138

formatted text panes. *See* editor panes

formatting classes, 37

function keys, 82

G

GIF (Graphics Interchange Format), 58–59

glossary, 205–217

gradients
> *See also* application graphics
> in button graphics, 71–72
> dithering added to, 61
> in icons, 65

graphic conventions in this book, xxi–xxii

graphic file formats, 58–59

Graphics Interchange Format (GIF), 58–59

graphics. *See* application graphics; button graphics; colors

grays, use in Java look and feel, 40, 42, 43, 44, 60

grids, 49–51

H

hand pointers, 79

handicaps. *See* accessibility

headline capitalization style, 46–47

Help button, 116

Help menu, 139
> About Application item in, 139
> mnemonics in, 90

help messages, capitalization of, 47

hierarchical menus. *See* submenus

highlighting, color design for, 43

Home key, 82, 87

HTML banners, 10–11

HTML editor kits, 172, 194, 200–201

human interface principles. *See* principles of design

I

I-beam pointer. *See* text pointers

icons, 63–66
> *See also* application graphics
> borders in, 64
> capitalization of text with, 46–47
> internationalization, 36, 62
> selection, 77, 80

implementation tips, defined, xxii

inactive components, spacing of, 48–49

inactive menu items, color design for, 43

inactive windows
> color design for, 41, 43
> example, 5

indicators
> for combo boxes, 156–159
> for submenus, 132
> for toolbar buttons, 144
> in tree views, 187

Info alert boxes, 123

informational symbols, 72

input focus. *See* keyboard focus

insertion point, 78, 80, 84

installation screens, 73

internal frames, 108–110
> color design for, 40–41
> keyboard operations for, 193–194

internationalization, 33–37
> fonts and, 37
> formatting classes and, 37
> graphics and, 36, 62
> JDK support for, 17
> layout managers and, 35, 49
> mnemonics and, 33, 36
> placement of checkbox text, 154
> placement of radio button text, 155
> recommended reading, xxvi–xxvii
> resource bundles and, 35, 164
> scrollbars and, 104
> Stop button and, 122
> testing in different locales, 37
> text handling and, 17, 35–37, 49, 52

internationalization guidelines, defined, xxii

J

JApplet component. *See* applets
Java 2 SDK, 15-16
Java 2D API, 16
Java Accessibility API, 16
    See also accessibility
Java Accessibility Utilities, 16
Java applets. *See* applets
Java Development Kit (JDK), 15-16
Java Foundation Classes (JFC)
    downloading with applets, 28
    features of, 15-18
    table of major JFC components, 19-22
Java look and feel
    color model, 39-44
    compared to other designs, 23-24
    defined, 15
    design fundamentals, 3-4
    fonts in, 45
    keyboard operations in, 82-90
    mouse operations in, 77-82
    visual tour of, 4-13
Java look and feel standards, defined, xxi
JavaHelp, 139
JButton component. *See* command buttons;
    toolbar buttons
JCheckbox component. *See* checkboxes
JCheckboxMenuItem component. *See* checkbox
    menu items
JColorChooser component. *See* color choosers
JComboBox component. *See* combo boxes
JDesktopPane component. *See* desktop panes
JDialog component. *See* dialog boxes
JDK (Java Development Kit), 15-16
JEditorPane component. *See* editor panes
JFC. *See* Java Foundation Classes
JFrame component. *See* primary windows
JInternalFrame component. *See* internal frames
JLabel component. *See* labels
JList component. *See* lists
JMenu component. *See* drop-down menus;
    submenus
JMenuBar component. *See* menu bars

JMenuItem component. *See* menu items
Joint Photographic Experts Group (JPEG), 58, 73
JOptionPane component. *See* alert boxes
JPanel component. *See* panels
JPasswordField component. *See* password fields
JPEG (Joint Photographic Experts Group), 58, 73
JPopupMenu component. *See* contextual menus
JProgressBar component. *See* progress bars
JRadioButton component. *See* radio buttons
JRadioButtonMenuItem component. *See* radio
    button menu items
JScrollBar component. *See* scrollbars
JScrollPane component. *See* scroll panes
JSeparator component. *See* separators
JSlider component. *See* sliders
JSplitPane component. *See* split panes
JTabbedPane component. *See* tabbed panes
JTable component. *See* tables
JTextArea component. *See* text areas
JTextField component. *See* text fields
JTextPane component. *See* editor panes
JToggleButton component. *See* toggle buttons
JToolBar component. *See* toolbars
JTooltip component. *See* tool tips
JTree component. *See* tree views
JWindow component. *See* plain windows

K

key bindings. *See* keyboard operations
keyboard focus, 83-85
    accessibility and, 32, 83-85
    defined, 83
keyboard navigation and activation. *See* keyboard
    operations
keyboard operations, 83-90
    See also keyboard shortcuts; mnemonics
    for navigation and activation, 85-87
    tables of, 191-203
keyboard shortcuts, 87-88
    See also keyboard operations; mnemonics
    defined, 83
    duplicates in contextual menus, 140
    duplicates in toolbar buttons, 145

example, 7
font design for, 45
in tool tips, 144
style in menus, 88, 130
table of common sequences, 88
keys
Alt, 82, 88–89
arrow, 82, 85, 86, 191
Backspace, 82
Command, 87
Control, 7, 80, 82–88, 191
Delete, 82
End, 82, 87
Enter and Return, 82, 86, 87, 149
Escape, 87, 89, 150
function, 82
Home, 82, 87
Meta, 87
modifier, 82, 85–89
Option, 82
Page Down, 82, 86
Page Up, 82, 86
Shift, 80, 82, 85, 191
spacebar, 85, 87
Tab, 85, 86, 191

L

labels, 164–166
See also text
active and inactive, 165
capitalization of, 46–47
color design for, 40–41, 43
communicating status with, 166
example, 9
identifying controls with, 164–166
internationalization and, 52
mnemonics in, 166
spacing and alignment of, 52, 53, 165
layers. *See* containers
layout managers, 35, 49, 101
layout. *See* spacing and alignment
legal requirements
About boxes, 76
accessibility and, 30
splash screens, 75

list boxes. *See* combo boxes
lists, 173–175
keyboard operations for, 195
scrolling in, 174
selection in, 80, 174–175
localization, 33–37
See also internationalization
login dialog boxes, 120
login splash screens, 75
look and feel designs, 23–24
See also Java look and feel
lower-level containers, 101–108
See also panels; scroll panes; split panes; tabbed panes

M

Macintosh look and feel, 24
MDI (multiple document interface), 108–110, 112
menu bars, 130–131
in applets, 29
example, 6
keyboard operations for, 196
menu items, 132–136
See also keyboard shortcuts; menus; mnemonics
About Application (Help menu), 139
available and unavailable, 133
capitalization of, 46
checkbox, 135
choosing, 133
Close (File menu), 98, 137
color design for, 40–41, 42, 43, 130
ellipsis mark in, 134
example, 7
Exit (File menu), 98, 137
highlighted, 133
keyboard operations for, 196
Preferences (File menu), 134
radio button, 136
in submenus, 132
table of common keyboard shortcuts, 88
table of common mnemonics, 90
menu separators, 7, 134, 136
menu titles, 131
See also keyboard shortcuts; menu items; menus; mnemonics

menu titles (*continued*)
   capitalization of, 46
   color design for, 40–41, 42, 43, 130
   example, 6
   font design for, 45
   order of, 136
menus, 129–146
   See also contextual menus; drop-down menus;
     keyboard shortcuts; menu bars; menu items;
     menu titles; mnemonics; submenus
   applets and, 29
   choosing items, 133
   color design for, 40–41, 42, 43, 130
   common in Java look and feel, 136–139
   displaying, 131
   Edit, 7, 88, 90, 138
   ellipsis mark in, 134
   File, 88, 90, 134, 137
   Format, 7, 138
   Help, 90, 139
   keyboard operations for, 196
   Object, 137
   order of, 136
   separators, 7, 134, 136
   types of, 129
   View, 139
Meta key, 87
Metal. *See* Java look and feel
MetalEdit application, 5–10
Microsoft Windows look and feel, 24
MIME (Multipurpose Internet Mail Extensions), 82
minimized internal frames, 109–110, 193
minimized windows, example, 5
mnemonics, 88–90
   See also keyboard operations; keyboard shortcuts
   accessibility and, 31–32, 88–90
   in applets, 29
   defined, 83
   in dialog boxes, 113
   examples, 7, 9
   international considerations, 33, 36
   in labels, 9, 166
   table of common assignments, 90
modal dialog boxes, 112
modeless dialog boxes, 112

models (in components), 17–18
modifier keys, 82, 85–89
   See also keyboard shortcuts; mnemonics
mouse buttons, 77–78
mouse operations, 77–82
   See also dragging
   clicking, 77–78, 80
   displaying contextual menus, 80–81
mouse-over feedback, 79, 145
move pointers, 79
multiplatform design, recommended reading, xxvi
multiple document interface (MDI), 108–110, 112

N
navigation, 85–87
   See also keyboard shortcuts; mnemonics
   accessibility considerations, 31, 32
   between components, 191
   tab traversal, 32, 114
   tables of keyboard operations, 191–204
nested panes, 106, 107–108
nodes, in tree views, 187–188
noneditable combo boxes, 157–158
   See also combo boxes
noneditable text fields, 167
   See also text fields

O
Object menu, 137
OK button, 116–117
option buttons. *See* radio buttons
Option key, 82

P
padding. *See* spacing and alignment
Page Down key, 82, 86
Page Up key, 82, 86
palette windows, 110
   See also dialog boxes
palettes, color, 58, 59, 60
   See also color choosers; colors
panels, 51–52, 101

panes. *See* scroll panes; split panes; tabbed panes

password fields, 168–169

plain windows, 73–75, 99–100

platform-specific design, recommended
   reading, xxiv–xxvi

pluggable look and feel architecture, 17–18
   See also Java look and feel

plug-in editor kits. *See* editor panes

pointers, 78–79
   changing shape of, 54, 78, 82, 106
   table of JDK types, 79

pop-up menus. *See* combo boxes; contextual menus

pop-up windows. *See* dialog boxes

posting menus, 131, 133

pre-dithered gradients, 60–61, 65, 71–72
   See also application graphics

preferences dialog boxes, 9, 113–114, 120–121

Preferences item (File menu), 134

primary colors, in Java look and feel, 40–41, 43–44

primary windows, 95–98
   See also windows
   defined, 93
   platform-specific examples, 5, 6

principles of design, 27–37
   accessibility, 30–32
   applets and, 28–29
   internationalization and, 33–37
   recommended reading, xxii–xxiii

print dialog boxes, 121

product names, 74, 76

progress bars, 160–161
   color design for, 40–41
   defined, 147

progress dialog boxes, 55, 121–122

progress feedback, 54, 121–122, 160–161
   See also feedback

Q

Question alert boxes, 125–126

Quit. *See* Exit item

R

radio button menu items, 135–136
   example, 7
   keyboard operations for, 196

radio buttons, 155–156
   capitalization of text with, 47
   example, 9
   keyboard operations for, 196
   in menus, 135–136
   spacing of, 156

reading order and localization, 35

recommended reading, xxii–xxviii

Reset button, 118

resize pointers, 79

resource bundles, 35, 164

Retirement Savings Calculator applet, 10–13

Return key, 82, 86, 87, 149

reverse video, 43

rollovers. *See* mouse-over feedback

rows in tables
   selecting, 182–184
   sorting, 179

RTF editor kit, 171

S

screen readers, 16
   See also accessibility

scroll arrows, 103–104

scroll boxes, 102
   color design for, 40–41
   example, 8

scroll panes, 8, 102–103, 169–170

scrollbars, 102–104
   example, 8
   in lists, 174
   in tables, 177
   internationalization considerations, 104
   keyboard operations for, 197

secondary colors, in Java look and feel, 40, 41–42,
   43–44

secondary menus. *See* submenus

secondary windows, 93, 98–99
   See also dialog boxes

security of information, in applets, 28–29
selection, 77, 80
    of list items, 174–175
    of table cells, 180–182
    of table columns, 184–186
    of table rows, 182–184
sentence capitalization style, 47
separators, 7, 134, 136
shadows, color design for, 41, 43
Shift key, 80, 82, 85, 191
shortcut keys. *See* keyboard shortcuts
shortcut menus. *See* contextual menus
sliders, 159–160
    capitalization of text with, 47
    defined, 147
    drag texture in, 85
    example, 12
    keyboard operations for, 197
small type style, in Java look and feel, 43, 45
sorting order and localization, 37
spacebar, 85, 87
spacing and alignment, 47–53
    in alert boxes, 122
    inside button graphics, 66–72
    of checkboxes, 48–49, 154–155
    of command buttons, 122–123, 151
    between components, 48–49
    design grids and, 49–50
    in dialog boxes, 50–51, 115
    internationalization and, 49
    of labels, 52, 53, 165
    layout managers and, 35, 49, 101
    of radio buttons, 156
    of scrollbars, 103
    in tables, 177
    of text, 49, 52–53
    of titled borders, 51–52
    of toggle buttons, 152–153
    of toolbar buttons, 143
splash screens, 73–75, 99–100
split panes, 106–108
    drag texture in, 85
    keyboard operations for, 198
splitter bars, 107
standard menus. *See* drop-down menus

Stop button, 122
styled text editor kit, 170–171, 200–201
submenus, 132
    See also menus
    defined, 129
    keyboard operations for, 196
Swing. *See* Java Foundation Classes
symbols, 62
system colors, 59
system status feedback, 55
system type style, in Java look and feel, 43, 45

T

Tab key, 85, 86, 191
tab traversal, 32, 114
tabbed panes, 104–106
    capitalization of tab names, 47
    keyboard operations for, 198
tables, 176–186
    cell background color, 176
    editing cells, 177
    example, 12
    font design for, 45
    format options, 177
    keyboard operations for, 199–200
    reordering columns, 177
    resizing columns, 178–179
    scrolling in, 177
    selecting cells, 180–182
    selecting columns, 184–186
    selecting rows, 182–184
    selection techniques in, 80
    sorting rows, 179
text, 163–172
    See also editor panes; fonts; labels; password
        fields; text areas; text fields
    in buttons, 143, 149, 151
    capitalization in interface, 46–47
    color design for, 43
    direction of, 17
    internationalization and, 17, 34–37, 49, 52
    selection, 77, 80
    spacing and alignment, 49, 52–53
    use in labels, 52

text areas, 169–170, 200–201
text fields, 167–168
    capitalization of labels with, 47
    in combo boxes, 158, 159
    examples, 9, 12
    font design for, 45
    keyboard operations for, 202
    in sliders, 160
text pointers, 79
themes, 23, 39–45
three-dimensional effects. *See* flush 3D effects
title bars
    alert box examples, 10
    capitalization of text in, 47
    color design for, 41, 43
    dialog box examples, 9
    dragging, 109
    window examples, 6
titled borders, 51–52
toggle buttons, 152–153
    See also button graphics; command buttons;
      toolbar buttons
    example, 8
    keyboard operations for, 202
tool tips, 145–146
    capitalization of, 47
    font design for, 45
    keyboard operations for, 203
    timing of, 146
    for toolbar buttons, 144
toolbar buttons, 142–145
    See also button graphics; command buttons;
      toggle buttons
    examples, 6, 8
    graphics in, 66–67
    with menus, 144
    spacing of, 143
    text in, 143
    tool tips for, 143
toolbars, 140–145
    docking, 141–142
    examples, 6, 8
    keyboard operations for, 203
    spacing of buttons in, 143
    tool tips for, 144

top-level containers, 97–100
    See also dialog boxes; plain windows; primary
      windows; utility windows
trademarks, 74, 76
translating text, 34–36, 49, 52, 122
tree views, 187–189
    font design for, 45
    keyboard operations for, 203–204
triangles. *See* indicators
triple-clicking, 77, 80
turners, 187–188
type styles, in Java look and feel, 45
typography. *See* fonts; text

U
unavailable items in menus, 133
usability testing
    accessibility issues, 32
    internationalization, 37
user type style, in Java look and feel, 43, 45
utility windows, 100
    defined, 93
    keyboard operations for, 194

V
version numbers, in About box, 76
vertical spacing. *See* spacing and alignment
View menu, 139
visual design, 39–55
    See also application graphics; spacing and
      alignment
visual identifiers, product, 74, 76

W–Y
wait pointers, 79
Warning alert boxes, 10, 124
warning symbols, 72
web. *See* applets
web-safe colors, 58, 60
white, use in Java look and feel, 40, 42, 43, 44

window controls
    close controls, 98, 99, 109, 110
    in internal frames, 108–109
    in plain windows, 99–100
    platform-specific examples, 6
    in primary windows, 97–98
windows, 93–110
    See also dialog boxes
    active, 5, 40, 43
    browser, 5, 10–13, 29
    capitalization of titles, 47
    color design for, 40–41, 43
    frames and, 22
    keyboard focus, 83
    keyboard operations for, 193–194
    in MDIs, 108–110

    palette, 110
    panels and panes in, 51–52, 101–108
    plain, 73–75, 99–100
    platform-specific examples, 5, 6
    primary, 93, 95–98
    secondary, 93, 98–99
    as top-level containers, 97–100
    utility, 93, 100
Windows. *See* Microsoft Windows look and feel
word order and localization, 36
word wrap, in text areas, 169–170

Z
zoom box. *See* window controls
zooming panes, 107

Colophon

LEAD WRITER
Patria Brown

WRITERS
Patria Brown, Gail Chappell

LEAD HUMAN INTERFACE DESIGNER
Don Gentner

JAVA LOOK AND FEEL CREATOR
Chris Ryan

MANAGING EDITOR
Sue Factor

GRAPHIC DESIGNER
Gary Ashcavai

ILLUSTRATORS
Gary Ashcavai, Don Gentner, Chris Ryan

PRODUCTION EDITOR
Bob Silva

PRODUCT MARKETING MANAGER
Christine Bodo

MANAGEMENT TEAM
Laine Yerga, Lynn Weaver, Rob Patten

GUIDELINE CONTRIBUTORS
Don Gentner, Chris Ryan, Michael C. Albers, Brian Beck, David-John
Burrowes, Carola Fellenz, Robin Jeffries, Earl Johnson, Jeff Shapiro,
Dena Shumila

Special thanks to Jonathan Schwartz and the Enterprise Products
Group in Java Software

Grateful acknowledgments to Ruth Anderson, Maria Capucciati,
Tom Dayton, Martine Freiberger, Janice Gelb, Dale Green, Mary
Hamilton, George Kaempf, Andrea Mankoski, Anant Kartik Mithal,
Moggy O'Donovan, Ray Ryan, Scott Ryder, Tom Santos, the Swing
Team, Harry Vertelney, Willie Walker, Steve Wilson, and all our
internal and external reviewers

This manual was written on Sun Microsystems workstations using
Adobe® FrameMaker software. Final page negatives were output
directly from text files on an AGFA Avantra 44 imagesetter. Line art
was created using Adobe Illustrator. Screen shots were edited in
Adobe Photoshop.

Text type is SunSans and bullets are ITC Zapf Dingbats. Courier is
used for computer voice.